How the Soul
WAS WON

REV. RICHARD STACKHOUSE

ISBN 979-8-89243-210-8 (paperback)
ISBN 979-8-89243-211-5 (digital)

Copyright © 2024 by Rev. Richard Stackhouse

All rights reserved. No part of this publication may be reproduced, distributed, or transmitted in any form or by any means, including photocopying, recording, or other electronic or mechanical methods without the prior written permission of the publisher. For permission requests, solicit the publisher via the address below.

Christian Faith Publishing
832 Park Avenue
Meadville, PA 16335
www.christianfaithpublishing.com

Printed in the United States of America

"Create in me a clean heart, O God, and renew a steadfast spirit within me. Do not cast me away from Your presence, and do not take Your Holy Spirit from me. Restore to me the joy of Your salvation and uphold me *by Your* generous Spirit. *Then* I will teach transgressors Your ways, and sinners shall be converted to You."
—Psalms 51:10–13 (NKJV); italics added

PREFACE

I have chosen to write for the glory of God. This book is not about theological directions or interpretations, and it is not about church dogmas. Nevertheless, the reader will hear some of the spiritual influences of the author's life, and that may reflect a particular theology or church structure.

How the Soul Was Won is kind of a play on the theme "how the West was won." I am no expert on the history of the movement westward. Although, from some of the books I have read and movies I have watched, the West didn't think it needed to be won. So the experts on these subjects would teach you more. My point here is in the same way that the West didn't think it needed to be won, the soul, too, doesn't think it needs to be won. The major difference here is that the West takeover wasn't gracious. The soul has been won by God from the beginning with grace and love. And yet there are similar battles of resistance.

I have grown up in a conservative community in upstate New York, and my family may have been the front-runners of developing that community's mindset. I am the youngest of six children, fulfilling that role when I have been born thirty minutes later than my twin brother. And this leads me to the title of the book: *How the Soul Was Won*. God has begun a work in me, and for a good portion of my life, I have been unaware of God's work and have had very little guidance in the spiritual arenas. And that has not deterred God from his process of winning my soul.

God has made me a messenger to let the world know that my soul has been won and that he has won the souls of the rest of the world. After graduating Bible college and seminary, I have been ordained and have served as a pastor and chaplain for over twenty years. During these years, I have witnessed God winning the soul and experienced my life being made more whole in the presence of God.

During the process of education and spiritual growth I have experienced varied connections with people that helped develop my faith—Benedictine monks, Methodist professors, Lutheran pastors, and Episcopal and Catholic priests. I have studied mysticism, some Buddhism, some Islam, and other world religions. Many of the people that I have met seemed to be experiencing confusion and frustration about God and their relationship of faith, like King Solomon in the following verse: "God has made everything beautiful in its time. He has also set eternity in the hearts of men, yet they cannot fathom the work that God has done from beginning to end" (Ecclesiastes 3:11).

King Solomon has had the pleasures of the world at his fingertips. It has been said at one time he have had all the fortune he wanted—world leaders seeking his counsel—but that hasn't satisfied him. He wanted something more. His heart and soul have moved from having much to feeling poor. Then he has returned to thinking about the God who has spoken to him at the beginning of his reign. When everything seems to be meaningless, God provides the meaning we need and the courage to tell others. In Solomon's case, the whole world knows his dark and enlightened moments.

"Meaningless! Meaningless!" says the Teacher. "Utterly meaningless! Everything is meaningless" (Ecclesiastes 1:2). In Solomon's despair, God has arrived and won peace for his soul.

God has won your soul. And this book will unpack that victory. It is a journey of sorts through some of the ups and downs of life in this world.

CONTENTS

1: The Quest for You 1
2: Running the Race 12
3: More Ways than One? 24
4: Stopping Our Tracks 34
5: The Opening 52
6: Where Am I? 70
7: Who Am I? 83
8: Under the Son 93
9: The Weight Is Lifted 116
10: Multiple Grace 126
11: All Aboard 136
12: A Peace of My Mind 151
Bibliography 171

This book and all my writings will be dedicated to the honor and glory of Almighty God. It is years of work from the Lord and Christ Jesus, who grafted me into his vine to produce fruit. And to God the Holy Spirit, I offer my deepest gratitude for your ever-abiding presence in my life. It is my humble desire as the author that this work be worthy of that dedication. And all efforts to accomplish such a project are credited to my wife and family, as they patiently traverse the roads of relationship with me and my service to God and his people.

To all the leaders of the Evangelical Methodist Church, thank you. To Rev. Kevin Brouillette, a superintendent of the EMC, I give my never-ending thanks. He has lit a fire in my soul and made me believe in church leadership again.

CHAPTER 1

The Quest for You

Now the tax collectors and sinners were all gathering around to hear Jesus. But the Pharisees and the teachers of the law muttered, "This man welcomes sinners and eats with them." Then Jesus told them this parable: "Suppose one of you has a hundred sheep and loses one of them. Doesn't he leave the ninety-nine in the open country and go after the lost sheep until he finds it? And when he finds it, he joyfully puts it on his shoulders and goes home. Then he calls his friends and neighbors together and says, 'Rejoice with me; I have found my lost sheep.' I tell you that in the same way there will be more rejoicing in heaven over one sinner who repents than over ninety-nine righteous persons who do not need to repent. (Luke 15:1–7 NIV)

The above text is just one of the examples of God's quest to restore the relationship between him and his people, you, and me. God's act of creation has begun so many years ago that it is impossible to put it into a human timeframe. God has never functioned under time as we know it; He has just dealt with it. God seeks his creation forever.

This is what really separates the person who is born only of the flesh from the person who is born from above (born again). Prior to when I have been born of the Spirit, I have been limited to worldly/fleshly information. Once my Spirit have been born anew, born from above, or born again—whatever phrase is most familiar to you—I then have started to understand that God has kept his eyes on me, is with me/us, and is reforming my heart, mind, and soul.

The Quest of God

Lost and spiritually lost are two extremely different matters of the person. In terms of physically lost, we have heard stories and watched movies a young boy, I remember watching the television series *Lassie*. It has been a common theme during that series that someone would get physically lost, and Lassie and the rest of about search and rescue. As the cast would manage through a dilemma finding the lost person, with the never-ending quoted phrase "Lassie, Timmy is stuck in the well." And recently, I have had the pleasure of watching a coastguard search and rescue enactment.

Unfortunately, children, ventures, and dementia patients do get physically lost in this world, and search and rescues are sometimes successful at recovery, but other times not. Most officials who lead a rescue for the lost seek the guidance of God for help. Have you ever prayed "God help me find my keys"?

Lost in the World

Let's move from the theme of the professionally trained rescue people who find the lost to the people who are lost in their worldly existence and who sometimes feel it and sometime don't. The paces and phases of our society are so implemented and demanding that a person finds themselves going through the paces not knowing why and what the goal is. Getting caught up in the rat race can easily produce another lost syndrome. Many college students find themselves away from home, family, and comfort that they get caught up into the rat race and feel lost and lonely. I have worked as a chaplain for a four-year college and have had countless conversations with students who have felt lost in the crowd and missed the families. This kind of physical lostness is tough on the emotion and spirit, even though you are where you think you are supposed to be. People move to a new location for work and experience some separation anxieties, and they often say, "I feel lost here." And if I can make you aware of this, I also need to make you aware that God knows more than I do about all this. Jesus called his disciples while they have been lost in their routine lives.

The Quest of God: Lost in the World

It is necessary to remember the words I prefaced with "Create in me a clean heart, O God." God is aware of the lost and hungry and provides a remedy for the sincere heart, mind, and soul.

> As Jesus went on from there, he saw a man named Matthew sitting at the tax collector's booth. "Follow me," he told him, and Matthew got up and followed him. While Jesus was having dinner at Matthew's house, many tax collectors and sinners came and ate with him and his disciples. When the Pharisees saw this, they asked his disciples, "Why does your teacher eat with tax collectors and sinners?" On hearing this, Jesus said, "It is not the healthy who need a doctor, but the sick. But go and learn what this means: 'I desire mercy, not sacrifice.' For I have not come to call the righteous, but sinners. (Matthew 9:9–13 NIV)

The text above reveals to us the insight of God the Father, the Son, and the Holy Spirit into the people who are physically lost in the world and the circumstances they have adapted to. Jesus has known that Matthew and many others have been needing something to break the lost patterns, feelings, and habits in their lives. He is the doctor who knows all of our needs even before we are ready to admit or recognize them.

In our current culture, people are more reluctant to go to church to find a way they can fit in after they have made a move or relocation. Just a couple of decades ago, when a physician moves into their first or new practice, it is suggested that they find a church and get anchored and acquainted with the new community. God has developed fellowship to remedy the lost feelings in a new place. In the words of Jesus, we are healthy when we know we need God and each other.

The Quest of God: Lost in the Spirit

"Doesn't he leave the ninety-nine in the open country and go after the lost sheep until he finds it?" (Luke 15:4 NIV). These words from Jesus are some of the most profound that are revealing of God's character. God does not want anyone to be lost—*lost* meaning "to not feel unworthy or out of grace."

God is aware of so much more than we could ever imagine. He is omnipresent, omniscient, and eternal. God is able to see all circumstances and is aware of all the thoughts, actions, joys, and fears of his people.

Why did the one sheep run away from the other ninety-nine? Was he/she immature? Was he/she resistant to structure? Was he/she afraid? Only God knows all the details of the human heart and soul, and he is not willing that anyone feel lost or perish.

There comes a time when we learn that God knows our spiritually lost circumstances, and he comes to get us. In my role as a chaplain, many people approached struggles and the end of life not knowing their eternal future, and they were spiritually lost. I have often become the means of grace that God uses to reclaim his lost sheep. It has not been my efforts that won the lost souls; it has been God Almighty living and acting through me. Many times, the words of Jesus recorded in the Gospels would come to my mind and mouth and provide comfort to the people. Many times, the words of the apostles and their letters would come to my mouth at just the right time.

God is claiming all of his children from every nation. We need to get over ourselves and the cynicism and skepticism of the world; they are not tolerated by God.

Step Away from the Cynical

Cynical is an adjective that means "believing that people are motivated purely by self-interest; distrustful of human sincerity or integrity." For example, "He was brutally cynical and hardened to every sob story under the sun, her cynical attitude." It can also mean "doubtful as to whether something will happen or whether it is worthwhile." For example, "Most residents are cynical about efforts to clean mobsters out of their city." It also used to mean "contemptuous, mocking." For example, "He gave a cynical laugh."

Another definition is "concerned only with one's own interests and typically disregarding accepted or appropriate standards in order to achieve them." For example, "A cynical manipulation of public opinion."

The above definition from the New Oxford Dictionary. There you have it. I have met many people who have allowed their thinking, faith, and character to be influenced by the cynics of the world. Cynicism comes in many shapes and forms and often has some roots in social experiences, family opinions, and prejudices.

The definition above paints a picture that, in one way or another, has influenced people. Lobbyists and others have used these tactics for political gain or manipulation for years.

The reason I mention this is that cynicism has corrupted my perception of God, the church, and God's people for many years. Therefore, I believe it is of the utmost importance that we step away from cynicism. If there is ever going to be a clear view of God—the Father, the Son, and the Holy Spirit—it is necessary to see the cynic in yourself.

In John 3, Nicodemus is a Pharisee, and he goes to Jesus at night to discuss the work of God and his perception of what Jesus has been doing. He goes at night so that none of his fellow Pharisees would see him, because most of them are cynics and have disregarded the evidence of God's work around them.

As I have stepped away from cynicism, I have enjoyed coming alive in the spirit, I have grown in faith, I have moved forward in character, I have accepted the role God set before me, and best of all, I have experienced his presence always.

This process has taken years to occur in my life, and yet it has only taken few moments in the hands of God to fulfill them. It is appropriate for the reader to understand that it is not I who write, but the Spirit of God within me.

Step Away from the Skepticism

Skepticism, according to the New Oxford Dictionary, is a noun that means "a skeptical attitude, doubt as to the truth of something." For example, "These claims were treated with skepticism." On the other hand, *philosophy* is the theory that certain knowledge is impossible.

Here is another word/subject that has corrupted the heart, mind, and soul of God's people for thousands of years. Skeptics, like cynics, put up a false wall of knowledge about God, heaven, and eternity. Skepticism, like cynicism, is an area of aloof ramblings from people who want to be right, but as certain, they are wrong.

The skeptic and the cynic would not exist if there has not been ample proof of something/someone to resist. In other words, every skeptic and every cynic would have no subject to debate if they don't believe there is the presence of God.

This the futile battle of the heart, mind, and soul. "I have seen the burden God has laid on the human race. He has made everything beautiful in its time. He has also set eternity in the human heart; yet no one can fathom what God has done from beginning to end" (Ecclesiastes 3:10–11). This is one of my favorite scriptures and sentiments from the heart of a man. Solomon, the author, has expressed his own uncertainty of the social, political, and religious view of the ways of God.

If we allow cynicism and skepticism to rule the way we think about the work of God the Father, the Son, and the Holy Spirit, then they will steal your peace and possibly the salvation God has offered you through the gracious work of Christ Jesus.

Are you getting tired of me bringing up subjects that attack your faith and peace with God? This is only the tip of the iceberg. Everyone needs to understand that the devil, the destroyer of the soul, and hell are real. I have learned about the existence of these during my experiences as a pastor and chaplain for people in the hospitals and the jail cells dealing with their personal demons that have been destroying their lives and eternal salvation.

A response I heard from a skeptic when I made a statement of faith was, "You, religious people, have gone off the deep end. Shut up about it." In other words, they were saying, "If we don't talk about it, it doesn't exist." Well, that is like saying if you don't talk about inflation, murder, stealing, pornography, and human abuses in many other forms, they don't exist. Raise your head out of the sand and recognize that evil, sin, and corruption do exist, and the devil wants you in his back pocket.

God sent the shepherd of the world to rescue us out of the hand of the devil. It is our opportunity to repent (turn into a new direction) and be added to the fold of God.

The most amazing and holy acts of grace I have experienced in my life has been my work as a chaplain. There have been hundreds of people that I would meet and speak with. I have been assigned people at random; they didn't pick me, and I didn't pick them. Picture the scenario: people are meeting me in some of the most complicated times of their lives—spiritually, physically, and emotionally—and they need support. And who shows up? A chaplain, a man sent from God. I have been always humble, receptive of their life experiences, and there to serve. Jesus has said, "I didn't come to be served, but to be servant of all." Find that scripture, and he will know you are serious. Those were amazing the miracles I have witnessed, the friendships I have enjoyed, and the love of God I have seen for everyone. Doubt, fear, skepticism, cynicism all belongs in the garbage. Jesus clears the Temple, so we can be the Temple of the Holy Spirit.

REV. RICHARD STACKHOUSE

The School of Hardheads

During God's quest for you and me and all the world, the paths his people take are often outrageous and painful, then by grace, they are finally redeemed. There are several examples in the old and new testaments about people allowing cynicism, skepticism, and hardheaded denial to cause them to turn from God.

> When the Jewish Festival of Tabernacles was near, Jesus' brothers said to him, "Leave Galilee and go to Judea, so that your disciples there may see the works you do. No one who wants to become a public figure acts in secret. Since you are doing these things, show yourself to the world." For even his own brothers did not believe in him. (John 7:2–5 NIV)

This is a conversation for you to imagine from Jesus's half-brother James: "I was caught up in my own jealousy and ignorance. This person [Jesus] so close to me could not be everything I heard He is. Are my eyes deceiving me? I see that He is holy, and still wonder why He is so special?" (A little poetic license.)

I was part of the school of hardheads. Hardheads differ from cynics and skeptics; the hardheads have the proof, and yet they refuse to see it or hear it. As the age old saying goes, "Can't see the forest through the trees." God challenges hardheads to repent. Jesus's brothers chose not to believe for a while that Jesus is the Messiah. Along the way and at the cross, that error has changed.

For the brothers James and Jude will say something like this. Jesus has always been there. We let our insecurities keep him at a distance and, even at times, had a sense of hate for his goodness/righteousness. Now I know better because his love for us overcame any distance, jealousy, and misdeed we had for him. I watch as this continues to go on in our society, families, churches, and synagogues. Do not be like my brothers and the hardheads. We charge you to recognize when God has sent his messenger to you and follow the Lord and Christ Jesus. James later writes as a leader of the church how his heart, soul, and mind have been renewed about Jesus.

The power of love and renewal are so obvious. Once James doubts Jesus and when he sees what Jesus has done for him and the whole world, all things are made new. That's you all too.

> Therefore, anyone who chooses to be a friend of the world becomes an enemy of God. Or do you think Scripture says without reason that He jealously longs for the spirit He has caused to dwell in us? But He gives us more grace. That is why Scripture says: "God opposes the proud but shows favor to the humble." Submit yourselves, then, to God. Resist the devil, and he will flee from you. Come near to God and He will come near to you. (James 4:4–8)

Acts 9:1–19 tells of the day when Saul met Jesus, Saul's conversion, and his new direction of life and ministry. Saul has been convinced of his new call, and he has changed his name to Paul. He has been a new creation. I could list scripture references and personal life experiences for the remainder of this book.

I know that God has called me to move you all through this process of his personal quest for you and your personal relationship with the one true god and father. The following verses reveal how it worked out for Paul.

> No, in all these things we are more than conquerors through him who loved us. For I am convinced that neither death nor life, neither angels nor demons, neither the present nor the future, nor any powers, neither height nor depth, nor anything else in all creation, will be able to separate us from the love of God that is in Christ Jesus our Lord. (Romans 8:37–39)

In the Heart of Every Soul

> Then God said, "Let Us make man in Our image, after Our likeness, to rule over the fish of the sea and the birds of the air, over the livestock, and over all the earth itself and every creature that crawls upon it." So, God created man in His own image; in the image of God, He created him; male and female He created them. (Genesis 1:26–27)

Many of the people I met have said something like this, "When I get to heaven, I have a bunch of questions to ask God." Are you one of those people?

I am sure that I/we probably have said something like that a time or two. We ask those types of questions due to the image of God that has been implied upon us, which has been changed by sin and the corruption of the world we live in.

During the life and ministry of Jesus, we see the image of God. He has calmed the storms, healed the sick, sent Peter to retrieve a coin from the mouth of a fish, and used the fish and loaves to feed thousands. Everything that the Word in Genesis 1 has said is fulfilled in Christ Jesus. Our likeness to God and our image to God are restored. Through faith in the work of Christ Jesus's ministry, his love for the world, and his suffering death and resurrection, we all can be restored as children of God.

Now what are some people waiting for? Do any of you think that by waiting for another piece of proof that God is with us you are being wiser? Are there subjects about life and death that you don't want to hear about?

Today I have given you the choice between life and death, between blessings and curses. Now I call on heaven and earth to witness the choice you make. Oh, that you would choose life, so that you and your descendants might live! (Deuteronomy 30:19)

God has called Moses as a prophet for the people of Israel to lead them out of their exiled life in Egypt. For those who are keeping God out of their mind, heart, and soul. you are fighting a losing battle. God has created every heart, life, and soul and sent Christ Jesus to reclaim his unclaimed children. You may say "I want to live my life and make my own choices," but your life is God's. Your eternity will be far more blessed if you let God manage the heart of your soul. Amen.

CHAPTER 2

Running the Race

Therefore, since we are surrounded by such a great cloud of witnesses, let us throw off everything that hinders and the sin that so easily entangles. And let us run with perseverance the race marked out for us, fixing our eyes on Jesus, the pioneer and perfecter of faith. For the joy set before Him He endured the cross, scorning its shame, and sat down at the right hand of the throne of God. Consider Him who endured such opposition from sinners, so that you will not grow weary and lose heart. (Hebrews 12:1–3)

The verses above are words inspired by God through the Apostle Paul and his friends. They have had come to the place of maturity in faith, which has developed their character to understand that heaven and earth are controlled by the hands of God the Father, the Son, and the Holy Spirit. The powers of God and the eyes of the saints who have gone before us all work for the cause of salvation for the world knowing Christ Jesus as savior and lord.

As wonderful and exciting as the above verses and comments are, we live in a world of false ideas and self-centered perceptions. Even the disciples have had their issues of pecking order and preference. We cannot run the good race that the apostle is referring to without putting God first in our life and thinking and knowing that God is at the finish line.

> Then the mother of Zebedee's sons came to Jesus with her sons and, kneeling down, asked a favor of him. "What is it you want?" he asked. She said, "Grant that one of these two sons of mine may sit at your right and the other at your left in your kingdom." "You don't know what you are asking," Jesus said to them. "Can you drink the cup I am going to drink?" "We can," they answered. Jesus said to them, "You will indeed drink from my cup, but to sit at my right or left is not for me to grant. These places belong to those for whom they have been prepared by my Father." (Matthew 20:20–23)

As we run this race of faith in the power of God, it requires a deep relationship with Jesus and an understanding of his character. Jesus has done what He came to do: save the world. He has not come to negotiate places and decisions for God the Father. We must get over our personal agendas and accept we are to be like Jesus. Jesus said, "I am the Vine, you are the branches, if you remain in Me and I in you, you will bare much fruit, but without Me you can do nothing" (John 15:5 NIV).

Running the race requires that we know who we are running the race with—as Paul says— "fixing our eyes on Jesus, the pioneer and perfecter of faith." The request that has been made in the Matthew 20 text, "I want one at your right and the other at your left," only has clarified their lack of knowing Jesus.

> When the ten heard about this, they were indignant with the two brothers. Jesus called them together and said, "You know that the rulers of the Gentiles lord it over them, and their high

officials exercise authority over them. Not so with you." (Matthew 20:24–26)

Running this race of faith requires that we know who we put our faith in. Is it Jesus or ourselves?

The gospel according to Matthew 20:20–26 reminds us of the world's influence over the disciples. The twelve have walked a ministry with Jesus for over three years. There have been times when they have been sent out to preach the gospel, heal the sick, and cast out demons. They may have been away from Jesus long enough to forget his character and humble demeanor. This is living proof that the gospel stories of Jesus's life and ministry keep us in touch with his character. The mother, the sons, and the mad disciples have displayed their ignorance about the character of Jesus. He does not show favoritism; the idea is offensive to him, not to mention that it hinders their relationships. Remember in Matthew 25 when Jesus sets the sheep on the right and the goats on his left. The sheep are saved, the goats aren't. What was this mother thinking?

Pride is not a requirement for running this race; as a matter of fact, it is a hindrance to running the race. If you have ever competed in a race or other sporting events, your typical interest is where you have placed—did I win, or did I lose? I've ran many cross-country and track meets as a high school student. I have not been a strong competitor and consequently have not asked "Did I win?" And yet I have always wanted to know how I placed in comparison to the number of runners.

> And the runners who have almost always been first are controlled by their desire to be in the best place. This is a human condition that permeates our lives, careers, and characters. Jesus has not chosen to be first; God has chosen for him to be first. Jesus has said, "Just as the Son of Man did not come to be served, but to serve, and to give his life as a ransom for many." (Matthew 20:28)

Do you know your own character? Are you willing to assess it? John Wesley would ask his friends, "How is it with your soul?" The implication being, Have you compared your character lately to the character of Jesus? And how is that working out? Therefore, running the race of spiritual life is not about a win in the track meet. It is eternal, and it requires the eternal presence of God the Father, the Son, and the Holy Spirit with us and within us.

Surrender

Come to Me, all you who are weary and burdened, and I will give you rest. Take My yoke upon you and learn from Me; for I am gentle and humble in heart, and you will find rest for your souls. For My yoke is easy and My burden is light. (Matthew 11:28–30)

When Jesus came to the region of Caesarea Philippi, he asked his disciples, "Who do people say the Son of Man is?" They replied, "Some say John the Baptist; others say Elijah; and still others, Jeremiah or one of the prophets." "But what about you?" he asked. "Who do you say I am?" Simon Peter answered, "You are the Messiah, the Son of the living God." Jesus replied, "Blessed are you, Simon son of Jonah, for this was not revealed to you by flesh and blood, but by my Father in heaven. And I tell you that you are Peter, and on this rock, I will build my church, and the gates of Hades will not overcome it. I will give you the keys of the kingdom of heaven; whatever you bind on earth will be bound in heaven, and whatever you loose on earth will be loosed in heaven." Then he ordered his disciples not to tell anyone that he was the Messiah. (Matthew 16:13–20)

These scriptures reveal our need to surrender our soul and intellect to Jesus in order to run the race and win eternal salvation.

I previously have written about running in track meets. If you have ever had the opportunity to run a relay race, you learn to depend on the other runners in the race. There are four. Just in case, you don't know what a relay race is like, here's a description: I would run the two-mile relay, and each runner has had a half mile course to run, starting with the first runner passing the baton to the next runner and on to the fourth runner who would finish the race. A successful relay team would decide to depend on one another and choose who would run which position in the relay.

The team will put their best runners in the first and fourth positions, hoping to ensure the win. I am usually third, hoping the first and second runners will provide enough of a lead so that I can maintain and pass the baton to the fourth and final runner, who is fast and strong. There is no room for pride or argument if the team intends to win. The team has a strategy.

Let's get really spiritual. God the Father has taken the first position, as creator, in this relay race with humanity, willing to put his image upon us. Genesis 1:27 says, "So God created mankind in his own image, in the image of God, He created them; male and female He created them."

God has stepped up first to reveal to the world his nature and character.

The world he created has existed far longer than we know or perceive. God put the perfect image of himself upon us for our benefit. Sin enters the human experience, and the perfect image of God is separated from His creation.

The second position in this relay race with humanity is Jesus. What sin and corruption has done to separate the world from the created image, Jesus has restored. The baton has been passed to Jesus to redeem the world for all who believe in the power of God revealed through Him. The Father has taken the first position and displayed his mighty power in all creation. The baton has been passed to the Son, Christ Jesus, who has displayed his power and victory over sin and separation from the Father.

The third position goes to the weaker: the believer. The believer soon learns that "when I am weak, he is strong." We need to get that God the Father and the Son have provided an awesome lead before they have handed us the baton. The Father and the Son are so far ahead because they have already secured eternal life for the believer. They have set it up so that all who believe in Christ Jesus win the victory.

The fourth position in this relay belongs to the Holy Spirit. Jesus has called us to surrender hand over the baton to the comforter and the counselor, the Holy Spirit. We will not win without the dedicated guidance of the Holy Spirit. The Holy Spirit keeps the lines of communication open between the believer and God the Father and the Son. The Holy Spirit convicts the believer. Have you ever had an aha moment when you realize you don't know as much as you thought or that you have never thought of it that way? This is conviction, which leads to insight, which leads to spiritual growth. The Holy Spirit will carry the baton until Jesus returns, and all heaven and earth are made new. I am ever grateful for the power of God.

I willingly surrender my baton to the Holy Spirt, that he may carry me over the finish line into the glorious kingdom of God. Come, O Holy Spirit, come create in me a new heart and a steadfast spirit.

Philippians 2:12 says, "Therefore, my dear friends, as you have always obeyed—not only in my presence, but now much more in my absence—continue to work out your salvation with fear and trembling."

> Life can be so unpredictable—joys and sorrows, beautiful blessings and distressing difficulties can come unexpectedly. Our life's dreams and plans can change in an instant. We all know this to be true. So how can we find peace amid such turbulence?
>
> Horatio Spafford knew something about life's unexpected challenges. He was a successful attorney and real estate investor who lost a for-

tune in the great Chicago fire of 1871. Around the same time, his beloved four-year-old son died of scarlet fever.

Thinking a vacation would do his family some good, he sent his wife and four daughters on a ship to England, planning to join them after he finished some pressing business at home. However, while crossing the Atlantic Ocean, the ship was involved in a terrible collision and sunk. More than 200 people lost their lives, including all four of Horatio Spafford's precious daughters. His wife, Anna, survived the tragedy. Upon arriving in England, she sent a telegram to her husband that began: "Saved alone. What shall I do?"

Horatio immediately set sail for England. At one point during his voyage, the captain of the ship, aware of the tragedy that had struck the Spafford family, summoned Horatio to tell him that they were now passing over the spot where the shipwreck had occurred.[1]

As Horatio thought about his daughters, words of comfort and hope filled his heart and mind. He wrote them down, and they have since become a well-beloved hymn:

> *When peace like a river, attendeth my way,*
> *When sorrows like sea billows roll—*
> *Whatever my lot, thou hast taught me to know.*
> *It is well, it is well with my soul.*[2]

Perhaps we cannot always say that everything is well in all aspects of our lives. There will always be storms to face, and sometimes there will be tragedies. But with faith in a loving God and with trust in His divine help, we can con-

fidently say, "It is well, it is well with my soul."
(Lloyd Newell, "It Is Well with My Soul")

The text in Philippians 2:12 emphasizes the point that this life and our eternal life are a work and walk that do not promise us a rose garden or peaches and cream experiences. The story above is what perpetuated the writing of the words of the hymn "It Is Well with My Soul."

The Apostle Paul's words in the text challenge his friends to obey the will of God in his teaching, preaching, and letters even in his absence. The letters remind people that he is not gone or unaware of their circumstances. He has messengers keeping him updated on the church's activities. In the same way, Paul would have wanted all followers of Christ Jesus to be aware that God is not absent or unaware of the human experience and current circumstances. God is with us. To accept this truth as Horatio Spafford has done requires the insight to whom you have surrendered your soul. This insight is available to everyone, although it does require "working out your salvation with fear and trembling."

I certainly remember the time in my life when I have been afraid to die. I have been afraid to die because I haven't known what it was going to be like. I have had only heard that there is a heaven and a hell. Heaven seems good, and hell seems horrible. I have had no idea what is going to be my afterlife. I have attended Sunday school for a short time as a child, where I had learned about Christmas and the baby Jesus.

As I have grown and I have learned about my personal demons, for lack of a better words, I have realized I had personal choices. When I obey my parents, they like it, and life is better. When I disobey, it is painful and unpleasant. Hearing words like "Remember God is watching you" has inspired the fear and trembling part. Then I have heard about prayer. You can pray to the god who sees all things and ask for help. My prayers have often sounded like "God, don't let Mom and Dad find out," not realizing what my actions have looked like in the eyes of God. My parents have not been able to help in this situation, so who do you talk to? My grandfather has been a man of faith in God, with a gentle soul, so I have tried to mimic him. Then the personal choices have come around again as a youth and teenager. Some of those choices have not been good at all. I have convinced myself that consequences were not a problem and that I will live and do what I could get away with. My point here is that we surrender one way or another. Surrendering to the will of the flesh causes a lot of problems.

What are the options? At fourteen years old, I have experienced God's grace through a pastor I have met in my time of need. Afterward, I said in a prayer to God, "I want to do that for someone too." And the words that have been spoken back to me said, "And you will." That has been the first step of surrender. In some ways, I had less fear; it seemed like I was in the hands of God and not ditched. It has taken many years and witnesses of God's people to clearly convince me to learn who Christ Jesus is, not just as my savior but to learn his character, commitment, and love.

Once, my pastor has said to me about this endeavor, "You want to be loved, then be lovable." Eventually, that has meant to me to fix my eyes on Jesus and I will feel his love. This has been my second step of surrender. I read the New Testament, then copied it, and started some Bible classes and courses. And my third step of surrender, at which I remain to this day, has come in the words of the scripture. In John 15:5, Jesus said, "I *am* the Vine, you are the branches. If I *am* in you and you are in Me, you will bare much fruit. But without Me, you can do nothing." It was God's call on my life through the words of the lord and savior, Christ Jesus. That has moved me through many Bible courses, seminary, and into pastoral and chaplaincy ministries.

I know whom it is that I have surrendered to. Running this race with Jesus requires us to surrender to him, because he has the power to save and transform our lives into eternal beings seated in the kingdom of heaven. And if you do any soul-searching and self-examination like me, you will find where you have taken control back from Jesus. Again, I surrender all. "All to Jesus I surrender, all to Him I freely give."

Perseverance

> As you come to Him, the living Stone—rejected by humans but chosen by God and precious to Him—you also, like living stones, are being built into a spiritual house to be a holy priesthood, offering spiritual sacrifices acceptable to God through Jesus Christ. (1 Peter 2:4–5 NIV)

These words from the Apostle Peter are coming from a heart of committed love and service to God and Christ Jesus. The Holy Spirit is the means of grace that inspires Peter to advance the cause of Christ Jesus, known as the Way. The Way, obviously the Way to God and eternal life. Peter has had his mountaintop experiences with Jesus, the high moments and then the low moments, like his denial of Jesus (Matthew 26:69–75).

God brings us back to our senses.

> When they had finished eating, Jesus said to Simon Peter, "Simon, son of John, do you love me more than these?" "Yes, Lord," he said, "you know that I love you." Jesus said, "Feed my lambs." Again, Jesus said, "Simon son of John, do you love me?" He answered, "Yes, Lord, you know that I love you." Jesus said, "Take care of my sheep." The third time he said to him, "Simon son of John, do you love me?" Peter was hurt because Jesus asked him the third time, "Do you love me?" He said, "Lord, you know all things; you know that I love you." Jesus said, "Feed my sheep." (John 21:15–17)

The last part of the race is not managed/run by us; it is in the hands of God. The above text reveals to us that God the Father and Christ Jesus have known there is more to Peter than sometimes meets the eye. We can read in the gospel according to Matthew and the others about the denial of Peter during the trial of Jesus.

Have Peter taken up the sword when Jesus has been arrested and have he agreed to know him at the trial, Peter would have been killed then too. A moment of fear and confusion has fallen over Peter, and his denial has saved his life for a later ministry in time. Jesus has reinstated Peter, and he has become a mighty preacher for God and perpetuated a movement still alive today. One of the attributes of Peter has, has been his willingness to remain with the disciples of Jesus, and he has grieved over the conditions of Jesus's death. His grief has become a fire of hope and delivered him from despair to perseverance.

Everyone will have this moment of meeting Jesus at the lake. In the text, Peter runs to meet and worship Jesus, and his life is transformed. Anyone can struggle their whole life long about faith, religion, and eternity. Some people embrace their faith and eternity early enough to enjoy it for many years. Others may put it off due to personal desires or embarrassment. Whatever the case, you are not the master.

Nevertheless, we all meet Jesus at the lake when this journey on earth is done. At the lake, Peter has found meaning and restoration for the remainder of his life on earth and then has been glorified to heaven for eternal bliss.

Making your choice is easy—choose life and choose Jesus. The sooner the better. It is glorious, loving, and eternal. Once you make the choice to follow Jesus and learn from the Holy Spirit, you are never left alone. Struggling with your life and your past may hang around for a period of time. When you accept Jesus as your savior, no struggle lasts forever.

In Revelations 21:5, it says, "He who was seated on the throne said, 'I am making everything new!' Then he said, 'Write this down, for these words are trustworthy and true.'" In Revelations 2:29, it says, "He who has an ear, let him hear what the Spirit says to the churches."

I am closing out this chapter with my words and a prayer that God has inspired from the John 21 text. As a measure of relationship, it is the disciples'/followers' option to work out the relationship with God the Father, the Son, and the Holy Spirit. Doing so will mark your name in the book of life for eternity. As in the experience of Peter, he may have missed the mark in the world challenges. Yet Jesus has known his heart is dedicated to God, and Peter's life has been made new. He also have gone a step further and has taken care of the people that matter to Jesus—"Take care of my sheep."

My prayer is this: Almighty God, my protector and redeemer, I ask you to protect and love the people I know and love and those people I do not know, because we all still belong to you. May your healing hand and your gracious spirit renew us all again and again, both in body and spirit. And as we all continue this life journey, bless us all today and forevermore. In Jesus's name I pray, amen.

CHAPTER 3

More Ways than One?

Paul then stood up in the meeting of the Areopagus and said: "People of Athens! I see that in every way you are very religious. For as I walked around and looked carefully at your objects of worship, I even found an altar with this inscription: *to an unknown god*. So, you are ignorant of the very thing you worship—and this is what I am going to proclaim to you." (Acts 17:22–23)

The above text reveals to us that all people have had a hunger to know what is beyond our current experience. This is a hunger that God the Father created in us. It's the power behind all relationships. The problems occur when we are ignorant of the relationship with God, which is available to all people. I personally have messed up a few relationships before getting to know God the Father, the Son, and the Holy Spirit. Therefore, if God is your first relationship, how much different the following relationships would be.

This is what leads us to the point of this chapter: people believe there are many ways to God and eternal life due to their vast experiences and relationships in this world. God is usually not their first relationship and quite often the last.

The Real Truth

In Genesis 2:7, it says, "Then the Lord God formed a man from the dust of the ground and breathed into his nostrils the breath of life, and the man became a living being."

In Jeremiah 1:5, it says, "Before I formed you in the womb I knew you, before you were born, I set you apart; I appointed you as a prophet to the nations."

In Ecclesiastes 3:10–11, "I have seen the burden that God has laid upon the sons of men to occupy them. He has made everything beautiful in its time. He has also set eternity in the hearts of men, yet they cannot fathom the work that God has done from beginning to end."

These verses of Scripture clearly indicate that God is our first relationship. As in the experience of Adam, God has been his first relationship. God has given him everything to survive. He only has restricted from him an experience he is not yet ready to handle. I can go into a long diatribe regarding how sin has come into Adam's life and the world, but that is not the point here. The point is that God is the first relationship of everyone in this world. God is there with breath that is needed at conception. Think about it: Adam and Eve has known no shame in the beginning because their first relationship has been with God. It is not until the third relationship has come into their lives (the serpent, Satan) that things have fallen apart in sin.

Nevertheless, we must acknowledge the plan of God. For thousands of years, religions have discussed their closeness or distance from their god and gods and prayed to them for their needs. That is so outrageous! The intention of God has not changed. It is the human perception of God that has changed due to ignorance, self-centeredness, and corruption.

The intention of God is that all people will know He has given them everything they need to flourish. God has given Adam and Eve everything they need to flourish and has instructed Adam not to take part of what will destroy him. God's plan at that time has been to care for Adam and Eve and their offspring/children.

Have there been no sin/corruption, then the experience for Cain and Abel would have been different.

> "Why are you angry," said the Lord to Cain, "and why has your countenance fallen? If you do what is right, will you not be accepted? But if you refuse to do what is right, sin is crouching at your door; it desires you, but you must master it." The Lord Who saw Cain in his mother's womb was there, the relationship he needed to flourish was right there. (Genesis 4:6–7)

Cain has rejected the relationship and the advice of God and sinned against his brother, and he has struggled because of it. God is the breath, the spirit, and the voice that everyone hears first, and that is the truth.

Like the words of God in Jeremiah 1:5, "God knew me in my mother's womb and directed my life." I will be the first to say, I wish I have had known that when I was young and growing. And it is not just for the prophet, priest, preacher, and messiah, but it is for all people. In my own life experience, I have not recognized the voice of the Lord until much later in my life. All the fears, mistakes, and problems I could have avoided. My parents haven't really known how God works in the womb and in planning stages of a person's life; therefore, they have not been able to teach me. And consequently, I haven't known this soon enough in my own children's lives to inform them. The miracle in this moment is that we don't have to be ignorant of this fact forever.

As a parent, have I understood what I know, I would have taught my children the greater truth of God. I am giving every parent an opportunity to be the parent God has called you to be. We live in a consumer society. Some of the products we consume are for our children in order to cope as a family. We give in love and generosity. And we all need to admit when we give in effort to appease the child (calm the beast). I did that too. It doesn't go well.

When God has given Cain and Abel to Adam and Eve, he has given them everything they need and kept them away from what they don't need. Think about it: when our children come home from the hospital, their needs are very limited usually. We feed them on time, we change when needed, and we let them sleep. (Obviously, I have seen exceptions to that rule as a chaplain when unforeseen medical circumstances occur.) There is a holy era watching over our baby. When they are awake, they smile beyond us, heavenward. Many of us experience something like I have described.

Newborns are often content and easy to care for. It is the peace of God that they are blessed with in the womb and thereafter. They are content in the first relationship that has God.

Then we want to cuddle them, but they are sleeping too much. We slowly and lovingly break the experience of peace. They don't need much at that point, so let them enjoy the presence of heaven. Then be patient as your child grows into the plan his or her Father created. It requires a very spiritual parent who has developed a close relationship with God. Don't you see that it is God's doing on what He wants for this generation also.

Now back to the title of this chapter, "More Ways Than One." I ask you to perceive how ridiculous that is. We have God, our first relationship, and everything after is dependent upon us knowing this as the truth. There is no other way. If you think that there is, you are lying to yourself and missing out on the best truth you will ever know. God the Father has created you, Christ Jesus has justified you, and the Holy Spirit sanctifies and lives in you.

The words of Solomon in the Ecclesiastes text reveals to us that God has been working with us and on us from the beginning. And the wonder of our soul will always hunger for the visions, the love, the grace, and the Spirit of God.

The Other Voice

> I charge *you* therefore before God and the Lord Jesus Christ, who will judge the living and the dead at His appearing and His kingdom: Preach

> the word! Be ready in season *and* out of season. Convince, rebuke, exhort, with all longsuffering and teaching. For the time will come when they will not endure sound doctrine, but according to their own desires, *because* they have itching ears, they will heap up for themselves teachers; and they will turn *their* ears away from the truth. (2 Timothy 4:1–5 NKJV)

The Apostle Paul's second letter to Timothy teaches the very subject that this chapter is about: people turn from their first voice, God, and seek after another voice that only feeds their own desires. This has been witnessed in the life choice of Cain. The voice of God is loving, teaching, and all knowing. Cain has heard the voice of God but has chosen to listen to a different voice, one that speaks to his own desires. Many people and Bible commentaries say that Cain has listened to the voice of the devil. That being the case, then everyone who believes there are more ways than one to know God are in fact listening to the devil.

The Apostle Paul teaches the way to God is with the Lord Jesus Christ, who will judge the living and the dead. The living is those who hear the voice of God. The dead are those who listen to the voice of the devil. Although this is a serious problem for every culture, including ours, God will not let it have the final say. As Paul charges Timothy with the tasks 'convince, rebuke, exhort, with all long-suffering and teaching.'

These tasks will be completed by the Holy Spirit of God living in the heart, soul, and mind of Paul, Timothy, and all who listen to the voice of God. These tasks are witnesses of the character of God. God will convince, rebuke, and exhort with long-suffering and teachings. God is long-suffering. It means that—in the voice of Jesus, the voice of God—"I will be with you always, even to the end of the age" (Matthew 28:20).

"*Because* they have itching ears." This is a syndrome. We can call it ambulance chasers, or we can call it political indifference, liberal apathy, television addicts, news and information overload, lust of the flesh, gossip, attention seekers, false media, and more. Once we tune our hearing away from God, we are opening ourselves up for evil influence.

Many people are more plugged into social media for its opinions, its misinformation, its hype, and its self-flattering gifts. I remember when my mother said, "If you don't have something good to say about someone or something, then don't say anything at all." Now there have been times when media has revealed something beneficial to the culture about corruption and a good Samaritan. Although sensationalism usually has top billing "because we have itching ears." We want to hear the bad news, the pain and suffering, the scandals, and the dirt on our next-door neighbor. This somehow makes us better than the challenge of suffering. You may think these comments are overdone or exaggeration. Turn on your television or go to your media search page, and you will find out more than you need to know about our corrupt society. The point I want to make now is, govern yourself. John Wesley would be asking you right now, How is it with your soul? If you are stressed out, perverted by the garbage you watch, then you may be listening too close to the devil. Occasionally something honorable is promoted by media, but often, God is left out of the matter.

"*Because* they have itching ears." Is there a cure for itching ears? Yes, it is the Gospel, the good news of the Lord and Christ Jesus. The Apostle Paul have said to Timothy, "Preach the word!" The Bible is a source of training, transformation, and relationship with God and his people.

We need to monitor our visual intake. Is it all movies, games, and media? If so, what you put into yourself will come out and cause problems more than you can sometimes handle and, ultimately, defile you before God and some of his people. Examine your life, what is good in it and what is bad in it. *Get rid of as much bad as you can.* That is the sanctifying power of the Holy Spirit's function. I will talk more about that later.

I always dread the election-year campaigns. In the recent years, there has been so little truth, and there is so much slander among candidates that it sickens me. How could a useful leader think and talk like that? When the prophets of the Old Testament has told the people to repent and speak what they have felt God called them to, they have been killed. Do you want to hear the Word of God? You may be tempted to say "No, you are a religious fanatic." I can assure you this from my experience as a pastor and chaplain that when you are leaving this world, you will want to hear the Word of God.

So why is it that we are so unethical, nasty, and corrupt? The words of the devil have had more time with you than the Word of God. I am not being judgmental; no, I am speaking from experience. Far too many years I listened to the ways of the world and not the voice of God and it almost cost me everything. I have listened to the public moral opinion, I have listened to people who are like a cult, and I have listened to sorcerers, but none of them has taught me how to be a better me. They are the voice of the devil.

The devil is a liar and focused on destruction. So many of these world groups are against God and the commitment of the Bible. The hard part about all this is when these people infiltrated the church. The good news has become the bad news, and lives have been lost. We have been tricked that Islam, which has arrived several centuries after Christ Jesus, was the way, but it is not. It is corruption. We can align with physics, sorcerers, political religions, and cults, but they will not lead you to God. I have met all of these and more as a chaplain and pastor, and in the end, whether it was death or transformation, it has been nothing but God the Father, the Son, and the Holy Spirit who has led the way for eternal life. I have had people say to me, "I don't believe that Jesus is the only way." Some of those people have thought that would discourage me and steal my joy. Nevertheless, when the compassionate power of God has arrived, they have received it gladly.

Getting distracted by the world, getting disheartened by some religious malice, and feeling challenged by your personal desires are part of the faith experience. All sunshine and no rain is not the perfect scenario either—take it from a Florida resident. This may be a time to remember the words *know thyself*. The most complicated part about people thinking or believing that there are more ways than one to God is accepting what you really want. When someone desires eternal life in the kingdom of heaven, it is all about a loving savior dying on the cross for the whole world; it is all about Christ Jesus. The gracious part is that God and Jesus are not unloving or unforgiving; they are redemptive and full of possibilities. Once a believer comes to the relationship of faith and truth, the plan of God and the workings of the kingdom are revealed. In the meantime, Christ Jesus is the way to the eternal kingdom of God.

Now for the person who does not know what they really want and who, in many ways, is contrary to thinking about faith in God or religious ideas, then other ways and lifestyles distract them. They are distracted in countless ways and directions. When a person plans a focus for their life and success, they are at time faced with time management choices or choices that are part of their plans. I have visited with people from many walks of life. Some are well-known Realtors, some are cardiologist, some are circus families, some are well-known financial giants, some amazing artist, some well-known attorneys, and some are homeless drug addicts, and yet all of them has lived their part of our society.

Each of these people have yielded to the directions that they have felt best would achieve their goal or desires. Physicians are drawn to medical teams and staff, and they focus their attention there. Money managers and circus families do much the same. We pick the circles in which we desire to run in, circles we have something in common with. During my years of jail ministry, I have seen the same.

My point is that more ways than one is not the truth regarding God; it is social and choice. When someone gets distracted or disassociated form God, it's time to know thyself, and that thyself is lost.

> "Do not let your hearts be troubled. You believe in God; also believe me. My Father's house has many rooms; if that were not so, would I have told you that I am going there to prepare a place for you? And if I go and prepare a place for you, I will come back and take you to be with me that you also may be where I am. You know the way to the place where I am going." Thomas said to

> him, "Lord, we don't know where you are going, so how can we know the way?" Jesus answered, "I am the way and the truth and the life. No one comes to the Father except through me." If you really know me, you will know my Father as well. From now on, you do know him and have seen him." (John 14:1–7)

This is a text that Jesus shares with his disciples and some of his closest followers. Jesus knows his earthly ministry would be challenging, and he wants to comfort the people. He also knows some people have been distracted with the opinions of the society, and he wants to help.

To truly know thyself is to know Jesus—God the Father, the Son (Jesus), and the Holy Spirit. That seems weird or outrageous to the seeker or nonbeliever. This leads us back to our being created in the image of God, the Trinity. We are created in the image of God, male and female they created us (Genesis). To fully know thyself is to know where you come from and where you are going. As I have taught previously, God said, "I knew you when you were in your mother's womb." You are God's creation, a child of God, and when that matters to you, it changes everything. You are no longer a temporary being, you are eternal. And that offers and challenges us to be more than we can be on our own.

God has sent Adam out of the garden of Eden due to his sin in the moment. Once Adam has had sin in his soul, God has known eating from the tree of eternal life would destroy him. He would be a sinful being forever.

Therefore, God has sent him away until the time when his righteous Son, Jesus, can come and take away the sins of humanity. Adam has had a "know thyself" moment too. It has occurred when he covers himself to hide from God. It is critical to have this moment. Twelve-step people surrender and say their lives are out of control, and they need the help of a higher power (God). Adam has needed that same help and now enjoys his eternal salvation because Christ Jesus paid for it on the cross.

You see just at the right time for each of us, God speaks to all of His children, no matter who they think they are, and God calls them out of darkness into light. People of all races and religions or nonreligions will fight this lure of God, and you will not win. The world/devil lures people into their weakness, but God lures you/us out of our weakness into strength. I have personally witnessed hundreds of times when God's Spirit arrives in the moment, and his child are transformed into a whole new life.

It is a total relief when someone takes the opportunity to let God in their life. Many of us have watched the crusades of Rev. Billy Graham, where people have walked forward to receive the gift of God and have been instructed to find a good church fellowship to keep the fire burning.

In Philippians 2:9–11, it says, "Therefore, God exalted Him to the highest place and gave him the name that is above every name, that at the name of Jesus every knee should bow, in heaven and on earth and under the earth, and every tongue acknowledge that Jesus Christ is Lord, to the glory of God, the Father." You can accept this truth: there is one way to live eternally.

CHAPTER 4

Stopping Our Tracks

> I am the true vine, and my Father is the gardener. He cuts off every branch in me that bears no fruit, while every branch that does bear fruit, he prunes so that it will be even more fruitful. You are already clean because of the word I have spoken to you. Remain in me, as I also remain in you. No branch can bear fruit by itself; it must remain in the vine. Neither can you bear fruit unless you remain in me. I am the vine; you are the branches. If you remain in me and I in you, you will bear much fruit; apart from me you can do nothing. (John 15:1–5 NIV)

This chapter deals with the grace of God that shows up in our lives. It stops us in our tracks when we are headed in the wrong directions. It reroutes us for a Christlike character and to love God and others. I have had those moments in my life when I have been stopped in my tracks, and a redirection arrived (like it or not.) In all cases, I have grown to like it.

Anytime something changes our lives abruptly, we respond in panic, fear, wonder, and sometimes despair. All the while, questions surface, and we paint a picture that often cuts us off from the success that lies before us. God stops us in our tracks because that is what it takes to get our attention and to help us change directions. We need to recognize evil circumstances.

My personal character is passive, and I want to be Christlike. I have been asked to accept a pastoral position in a very corrupt and conflictual congregation. The church is still in the midst of a lawsuit with a previous pastor when I have accepted the position. I have been interviewed by a UMC phycologist to determine if I have the skills to handle conflict. At the end of the interview, the phycologist says, "I would like you to be my pastor." The church and people have been a disaster.

My wife and I suffered more than anyone can imagine. The denomination has sold out to legal threats (the devil), and we have left after five years of hard work and service. Many people love us, and a few power mongers hate us. We stop the UMC and move on.

The point here is to know when to assess your current situation as unhealthy and move out of it sooner than later. I am a pastor who has a "never say die" attitude. I am a person with my cup three-quarters full. I strive for goodness as best as I can. I hang in there hoping to mend things until my life is threatened by the church leaders. I know this sounds outrageous, and I will never imagine such a thing have I not lived it. The hard part is, the leaders of the UMC say again and again, "It is not you. It is them." When peaceful resolve is met with threats and armed people, it becomes evil. These are people I visit in their hospital beds. I pray for them and their families, and I have survived their threats. I have been hoping for the best.

God has stopped me in my tracks and rescued me from that church and the UMC denomination. Stopping our tracks is sometimes a happy experience and sometimes a struggle. God knows how to do both. I have had those moments in my life when God has stopped me and said, "Today I do something new" (Isaiah 43:18). And I am so excited and am all in. And then, there are those moments when God says, "I am with you in all circumstance" (Matthew 28:20).

We can have the best intentions for serving God and His people; although, we do not have the omnipresent power of God to know when to escape in peace.

> But if you enter a town and they do not welcome you, go into the streets and declare, "Even the dust of your town that clings to our feet, we wipe off as a testimony against you. Yet be sure of this: The kingdom of God is near." I tell you; it will be more bearable on that day for Sodom than for that town. (Luke 10:10–12 NIV)

This text is a warning to the disciples of that day and also to us. Sometimes, we can believe we are doing great in a ministry, and other times, it's a lesson of grace. Are you giving the grace of God to people who don't care and, much worse, don't want it? If so, God will stop you and redirect your path.

You may not want to imagine a moment that God stops you in your tracks, but think of this: this is how Jesus works. He and the Holy Spirit are working together to make disciples of all nations.

On the previous personal witness of a horrible church experience for my family and I, there have been good and bad dynamics in the moment. I have wanted to believe I could fix their problems, but they have wanted nothing of the sort. Some people like disruption and chaos, and I do not. Some people thrive on disruption and chaos, and I do not. And that is how God taught me the difference of service and self-service. He has stopped me in my tracks and stopped the chaos. The important part is that we do not reject God's influence but prayerfully look for a new way.

The point of these witnesses is for the person who thinks that pastors and true Christians don't know the agonies that are part of our society. God stops everyone in their tracks. The intent is to turn the person in a new direction and give them a better life experience while we walk this journey on earth.

Our personal experience has been turned around and tremendously improved by seeking a denomination of the same faith and mindset, the Evangelical Methodist Church. There I have met people seeking ministry, service, and Christian love with no chaos. I have also taken a position as a chaplain for a medical team that appreciates my gifts and awards me with the "chaplain who made the difference" award.

It is important to remember that I am not a boastful person. I have had more hardships than I care to remember. I am a person who has experienced the watchful eye of God the Father, the Son, and the Holy Spirit and have been moved through the chaos of life with grace on my side. God loves me—in, though, and over the rough spots. And all heaven celebrates when one person wins and turns their life over to God.

> Meanwhile, Saul was still breathing out murderous threats against the Lord's disciples. He went to the high priest and asked him for letters to the synagogues in Damascus, so that if he found any there who belonged to the Way, whether men or women, he might take them as prisoners to Jerusalem. As he neared Damascus on his journey, suddenly a light from heaven flashed around him. He fell to the ground and heard a voice say to him, "Saul, Saul, why do you persecute me?" "Who are you, Lord?" Saul asked. (Acts 9:1–5 NIV)

There is no way I could title a chapter "Stopping our Tracks" without including this New Testament scripture. This book of Acts is authored by Luke, the same author of the gospel Luke. In both books, he is writing to a Greek leader named Theophilus. The gospel is a book to declare the life, ministry, death, and resurrection of Christ Jesus. The Book of Acts is about the church that grows as a result of Christ Jesus. In the above text, we learn about Saul, a Jewish Pharisee who has been trying to stop the movement/growth of the church of Christ Jesus.

Here is the interesting/outrageous part: the Jews and Roman authorities have thought it was a done deal when Jesus has been crucified and buried. There has been talk of a resurrection of Christ Jesus, and many witnesses have seen him alive and resurrected. Some religious and political leaders have crafted a story that he was stolen from the tomb. Saul, who has called himself the Pharisee of Pharisees, has helped to craft the false story. Considering he has been one of the major liars and persecutors of the church, who better to stop in his tracks? And Jesus have done just that.

Saul has been so convinced that only the Lord can do this, so he has decided to surrender and learn what he will be told to do. Saul has been so impressed and repented that he no longer wants to be known as Saul the Pharisee. He became Paul, the apostle to Christ Jesus. Saul has experienced a moment of blindness, and then his sight has been restored. The point is, How does the world blind you?

To the readers, this is the story of Billy Graham:

> In a time of penny candy, nickel sodas, hair tonic, blushing brides, travelling preachers, and Sunday suppers, people were optimistic and busy. With so many other things to do, most young people were not thinking about things like Christian service and dying to self. Although it is true that Billy Graham enjoyed having fun, there was more. Somewhere deep, something fundamental was working inside him.
>
> In May of 1934, the Christian businessmen of Charlotte, NC, secured permission to hold an all-day prayer meeting at the Graham farm. On that day, a prayer was raised—that out of Charlotte the Lord would raise up someone to preach the Gospel to the ends of the earth.
>
> It was in that year the previously reluctant Billy Graham gave his life to the Lord at a revival meeting led by travelling evangelist Rev. Mordecai Ham. At 16 years old, Billy Graham was about to experience the transformation of a traditional farm boy into an instrument of God.
>
> In the Woods: In a time of burgeoning modernism, of science and philosophy, Billy

Graham walked in the woods one night seeking God's direction for his faith. The answer? The Bible—sealed by a prayer: "Father, I am going to accept this as Thy Word—by faith! I'm going to allow faith to go beyond my intellectual questions and doubts, and I will believe this to be Your inspired Word." (The Billy Graham Evangelistic Association)

This is just one of the lives of well-known people who have been stopped in their tracks and sent to go into a new direction. You may be tempted to say, "Well, this is Rev. Billy Graham. He is not like me, and I can't do that." Good for you if you do say such a thing. You are not to be anyone else, but to be like Christ Jesus. God stops everyone in his own way. I have spent five years being involved as a pastor for jail ministries. It has not been my plan, but God's, and I will share that story later. And I have witnessed the many times God has stopped someone in their tracks.

I can imagine by this page that the idea of stopping our tracks is not about wiping out our footprints from the sand or snow. It's about a spiritual and emotional event or era that has caused us to stop and wonder what just happened. And those moments have a physical impact also; it changes everything.

What Is Your Track?

I know people that say "bless your heart," and it comes out of their mouth in every other sentence. Some people think that is just the sweetest thing, and other people think it is phony. It certainly has to do with the level of sincerity of the words when they are shared or displayed. The point here is not to determine the sincerity of this phrase; only God can do that. It is about the way we all differ in our expressions and behaviors. Some people are turned off by super religious talk, especially if they are not used to it or have not heard such talk.

Are you inclined to reach out to religious groups for inspiration, or are you turned off by such things? I have enjoyed my life experience in many churches, Bible college, and seminary immensely. I also know my life experience is not the same as other people. Therefore, consider the meaning of "don't throw the baby out with the bathwater."

The idiom "don't throw the baby out with the bathwater" is a warning not to get rid of something good or valuable along with something bad. Be careful that when rejecting something bad. You do not make the mistake of throwing everything out, including something valuable. It is often used to warn people against making hasty decisions that they may later regret. This is from NoSweatShakespeare.com.

I use this idiom to remind us not be to rash when it comes to our relationship with God. When we readjust our life, we must always keep God as first, and we cannot forget that the only eternal and lasting choice is with God the Father, the Son, and the Holy Spirit.

> As Jesus was walking beside the Sea of Galilee, He saw two brothers, Simon called Peter and his brother Andrew. They were casting a net into the lake, for they were fishermen. "Come, follow me," Jesus said, "and I will send you out to fish for people." At once they left their nets and followed him. Going on from there, He saw two other brothers, James son of Zebedee and his brother John. They were in a boat with their father Zebedee, preparing their nets. Jesus called them, and immediately they left the boat and their father and followed him. (Matthew 4:18–22 NIV)

This text is a reminder of the wisdom of God working to change people's lives and direct their lives for the better. These disciples have been stopped in their tracks. They have been face-to-face with the omniscient power of God, and they could not resist. The scripture tells us they have been fishermen and not religious teachers. For these disciples, there has been enough chaos in their lives, and they wonder in their souls to respond without challenge to God.

Holy Undeniable

This may be an area of spirituality that some people may misunderstand, will want to ignore, or disbelieve. When Jesus has spoken to these disciples, he has spoken with a spiritual tone that they cannot resist. The voice of God is thundering, comforting, challenging, and mesmerizing. Christ Jesus is God in the flesh. When he called his disciples, they have been drawn into a holy and spiritual plain. When Jesus have spoken to the Pharisees and other religious leaders, he has spoken to their current attitude. When they have challenged Jesus and when they tried to trick him with false settings (John 8:1–11), he has spoken to them, challenging them, and the religious leaders have walked away befuddled.

For the person open to Christ Jesus, there is an arena that occurs known as holy conversation. This is a place where the heart of God and the heart of his child meet, converse, and love.

Holy Ground

> Now Moses was tending the flock of Jethro his father-in-law, the priest of Midian, and he led the flock to the far side of the wilderness and came to Horeb, the mountain of God. There the angel of the Lord appeared to him in flames of fire from within a bush. Moses saw that though the bush was on fire it did not burn up. So, Moses thought, "I will go over and see this strange sight—why the bush does not burn up." When the Lord saw that he had gone over to look, God called to him from within the bush, "Moses! Moses!" And Moses said, "Here I am. "Do not come any

> closer," God said. "Take off your sandals, for the place where you are standing is holy ground." Then he said, "I am the God of your father, the God of Abraham, the God of Isaac and the God of Jacob." (Exodus 3:1–6 NIV)

Like Moses in this text, most of us are caught off guard when God reaches out to us. The burning bush in this text represents the eye-catching skills of God. God knows how to get your attention. Now if you are thinking God is trying to get your attention with a Corvette, Mustang, a BMW, or worldly distractions, I would encourage you to guess again. God typically uses moments that cause us to think both physically and spiritually.

Nevertheless, this is a representation of God communicating with his children. In this circumstance, God knows Moses has a love for his people, the people of Israel. And God uses the right moment, when no one is there to distract Moses, to speak to him, and he becomes one of the most famous prophets of God.

These are real words between God and Moses. I have had many people ask me, "Do you really hear the voice of God?" And after many years of listening, praying, and studying the character of God, I can say yes. God knows my heart, dedication, sincerity, and desires. And from that arena, we talk.

> But Moses said to God, "Who am I that I should go to Pharaoh and bring the Israelites out of Egypt?" And God said, "I will be with you. And this will be the sign to you that it is I who have sent you: When you have brought the people out of Egypt, you will worship God on this mountain." (Exodus 3:11–12)

The point of this text is to share a real conversation between God and Moses. Again, for all of the people who are seeking, wondering, and even doubting about communication and relationship with God, God longs to hear your voice again.

Suppose you are to doubt the existence of the sport baseball? I can say, "Well, that is an easy fix. Let me take you to a baseball game." The simple point is that you will never believe that there is such a sport such as baseball as long as you stay outside of the diamond/park. The same is true when hearing from God and communicating. You cannot stay outside of the Bible, church, study, worship, and fellowship and expect to know the voice of God.

Everyone's holy ground is different. Clearly, the Bible is the resource for establishing your holy ground, yet all people have a different purpose and role as God guides us. God does not need another man to go to Egypt to lead that group of people out. Although, God is calling men and women to listen to his call in their current moment.

I wish I could give any of you who are wondering about this a crash course on communicating with God, but I can't. It has been many years of prayer, study, believing in the power of God that has inspired me to listen. There comes a time when each person must put aside all their ignorance and doubt about God and live by faith. Martin Luther, one of the great leaders in the reformation, has had his own holy ground moment when he opened his Bible to the New Testament letter to the Romans 1:17, "The righteous will live by faith."

In Romans 1:17 it says, "For in the gospel the righteousness of God is revealed—a righteousness that is by faith from first to last, just as it is written: 'The righteous will live by faith.'"

For Martin Luther, it has been this scripture that has spoken deep into his soul, and it has set him free from trying to live a life focused on works and not faith. How does this faith work? This is the story of a struggling preacher, John Wesley.

> Peter Bohler was a young German Moravian Christian. John Wesley met him soon after returning from his failed mission to Georgia. Bohler was in London preparing to travel to America to do missionary work among the slaves. John Wesley looked after Bohler and some of his friends while they were in London. Bohler, who

was about 10 years younger than Wesley, spoke a little English. Wesley spoke a little German, but they found that they could speak easily in Latin.

Wesley confided to Bohler that he was thinking about giving up preaching because he had no faith. He said, "I need faith that will give me three things: peace in the face of death, joy, and victory over sin." Bohler encouraged Wesley to "preach faith until you have it. Then you will preach faith because you have it!" (Dave Hanson, "A John Wesley Moment: Peter Bohler")

Rev. Dave Hanson is a retired pastor and John Wesley scholar.

Whether Wesley is successful with this task is irrelevant. It depends on the person and the level of faith. Bohler's words are to set aside your personal issues and put your faith in God. Setting aside our personal issues means taking them off the priority list and putting faith in God first. That does not remove your issue, but it puts it into the right perspective. And if you pray, God will take the issue into consideration. Prayer is the means that by which an issue is shared with God. That means, you are not alone in managing the issue.

You can research both Martin Luther's and John Wesley's lives to learn more about their journey of faith. I can share with you the process that works for me to know and communicate with God.

First, God is better, stronger, and holier than you and me. I pray, "My Father in heaven, I praise your holy name. I pray that your kingdom will come and your will be done [right now] on earth as it is in heaven. Give me/us all we need for today. Forgive me my sins and help me to forgive those who have sinned against me. Let me not be led into temptation and deliver me from the evil one. For yours is the kingdom, the power, and the glory forever. Amen."

When I pray these words, there are long pauses where it is necessary, like in "may your holy name be praised." You can accept that these are words of instruction from your God. Allow these moments to be the way you communicate with God. Stop during each subject, and talk to God your Father in heaven. When you ask for forgiveness, get real and be truthful to God about your life. He already knows you and wants to improve your life. Make your prayers the realest conversation that you have ever spoken. God is truth, and we must be truthful too.

Some people have asked me what subjects are we not allowed to talk to God about. God is all knowing. He always knows what subjects are on your mind, and I believe some subjects that we avoid are brought to our mind for correction and insight.

For example, I do not like all the political chaos that is pushed down my throat by the media, especially during election years. I avoid it. Avoidance can be a form of denial. Denial can lead to lying to ourselves and losing peace in the soul. God will use people, family, friends, and social moments to get you to pray and deal with the issues you are trying to avoid. I don't like the current woke movement, but it became more relevant when it challenged my family.

Prayer time is a time to accept that the power of God's holy ground can reinterpret your life circumstances. The following psalm of King David causes us to realize how brief a life in chaos actually is in the eyes of the Lord.

> Lord, remind me how brief my time on earth will be. Remind me that my days are numbered—how fleeting my life is. You have made my life no longer than the width of my hand. My entire lifetime is just a moment to you; at best, each of us is but a breath. (Psalm 39:4–5)

The truth of holy ground is that God has the means for providing eternal life. In the psalm, David's words prior to the people are a confession of the things that has angered him. And the holy ground wisdom has caused him to realize, life is too short to waste time being angry and ineffective.

And I believe we need our own holy ground moment when we let go and let God. It is our call as a disciple of Christ Jesus to do all we can for God's truth and message of the Gospel of Christ Jesus. We are to have a competing voice, and I challenge us to have a louder voice than the world. All the outrageous, misguiding influences of the world about sexuality, they are the lies of the devil, and the devil will destroy all that is right and truthful using the mouth and minds of the world's outrageous teachers. The false teachers will perish. It is up to us to inform the world's students of the truth of God the Father, the Son, and the Holy Spirit.

These misguided people who have surrendered to the lies of the devil/world about their sexuality, their bodies, and their choice to destroy the image of God, which was given them, will have their holy ground moment too. There is no escaping it. We must all stand before God. On a note of amazing grace, we can always pray for a holy ground meeting for these misguided souls before the final moment. Therefore, in this brief moment of these lives, I will loudly claim the winning power of God in Christ Jesus, which redeems the life and returns the image of God.

Holy Truth

I shared with this audience that the presence and glory of Jesus has mesmerized the disciples, and they have responded wholeheartedly to his call. Everyone will have this moment too. I fortunately have dedicated my life to Christ Jesus and have already enjoyed some of those holy moments of being mesmerized by the presence of Christ Jesus.

> As I, Daniel, was trying to understand the meaning of this vision, someone who looked like a man stood in front of me. And I heard a human voice calling out from the Ulai River, "Gabriel, tell this man the meaning of his vision." As Gabriel approached the place where I was standing, I became so terrified that I fell with my face to the ground. "Son of man," he said, "you must understand that the events you have seen in your vision relate to the time of the end." While he was speaking, I fainted and lay there with my

face to the ground. But Gabriel roused me with a touch and helped me to my feet. (Daniel 8:15–18 NLT)

The above text from the Old Testament reveals the daring and honest nature of God that has been given to this prophet Daniel. You may choose to read all of this chapter and book, and I think you would do well if you did. Although, if you allow yourself to get caught up into the imagery and the end-time prophesies, you may very well miss the revelation of God interacting with his children. I have heard debates over the end-time images in this book and the Book of Revelation, and all too often the debate does not lead the people closer to God. When you put in your heart, mind, and soul a desire to know God and establish a relationship with him first, then the glorious images of God and heaven will be yours in truth.

Like it or not, this chapter is stopping you in your tracks. I don't know where you are in your life and faith journey, but I do know this God stops us as many times as necessary. It will go much better for us if we do not deny the heavenly guidance.

The Holy Image

After six days Jesus took with him Peter, James, and John the brother of James, and led them up a high mountain by themselves. There he was transfigured before them. His face shone like the sun, and his clothes became as white as the light. Just then there appeared before them Moses and Elijah, talking with Jesus. Peter said to Jesus, "Lord, it is good for us to be here. If you wish, I will put up three shelters—one for you, one for Moses and one for Elijah." While he was still speaking, a bright cloud covered them, and a voice from the cloud said, "This is my Son, whom I love; with him I am well pleased. Listen to him!" When the disciples heard this, they fell

> facedown to the ground, terrified. But Jesus came and touched them. "Get up," he said. "Don't be afraid." When they looked up, they saw no one except Jesus. (Matthew 17:1–8)

This is one of the most exciting scriptures for me. It reveals heaven and earth, God's voice, the glowing presence of the Holy Spirit, and the desire of Jesus to show this to his disciples. Now here is the stop you need in your tracks question. Are you a disciple of Christ Jesus? If not, then get to a Bible-believing church and learn about the glories that await you. If you are a disciple of Christ Jesus, then be honest with yourself, Has Jesus taken you up the mountain? This is not a heavenly drill, like a fire drill, or practice run of the emergency broadcast system. (If that still exists.) This is Jesus revealing to everyone who says in their heart, "I will follow Jesus up the high mountain."

Some commentaries on this text describe this as a one-time moment when Jesus has needed three witnesses to substantiate his role in the deity. Some use this text as a moment when we see the Trinity established. Well, those two comments I certainly agree with; although, it is the rest of the holy moment that I intend to share.

Matthew 17 says, "Jesus took with him Peter, James, and John the brother of James, and led them up a high mountain by themselves." Those moments in my life when I am led by the Trinity to separate from the routine and follow God have always left the imprint of their holy image upon my heart and soul.

On the Lent season of 2002, I have decided to do something more spiritual. And I have set aside some time to pray, meditate, and read the Bible out of the parsonage and church office. I went to a park in the hills of Pennsylvania. I have not planned on a mild mountain climb, and it has not been very aggressive. As I stare up the labeled pathway, I realize a gradual incline. I take my Bible and an ample supply of water. Along the pathway, I stop to read my Bible and pray. I have been focusing on the Psalms and the Book of John. As I continue, not really thinking of the incline, I have just caught up into the way the Bible words are feeling so real to me.

I have started the pathway at 9:00 a.m., and along the way, there always seems to be something beautiful and eye-catching for me. One is the beauty of a Pileated woodpecker—how the sun shines through the trees and casts a shine on its body. The bird pauses for a moment and enjoys the warmth. At another spot, I see a glistening stone and pick it up as a holy gift. At 2:00 p.m., I have reached another point to stop, read, and pray, and I realize I have moved up the incline. And there was a breathtaking view of the valley and the Susquehanna River.

At that moment I have been reading John 3, the conversation between Jesus and Nicodemus—"You must be born again." I have been very comfortable and confident in my born-again experience in my life at the time. And then I have thought, *This is a living word active and transforming all the time; there was nothing wrong with feeling I was born anew in that moment.* I read and I pray and praise God for the beauty of his creation and inspired feelings.

The "stopping me in my tracks" moment for that day is yet to come. After praying and reading more, I get this daring sense in my soul to speak to God in a way I have never considered before. I ask in a prayer while I look over the glorious valley. I said, "God, why can I not stop thinking about you? What is it about me that I can't get you off my mind?" Thoughts like "Am I different?" "Am I special?" and "What is all this all about?" are going through my mind.

And then God says, "What makes you think it's you thinking about me and not me thinking about you." I am stunned, mesmerized, and praising God. All these years later, writing this still makes me choked up and in deeper love with God. The best part now is that all these years later, I know I am not different. I am loved by God the Father, the Son, and the Holy Spirit, who leads people to the glorious places to experience this love. These are the moments that cause me to know that God put me on this earth just as I am and only intends to make me into someone more loveable. Don't mess with the image of God he has given you. Ask God to examine and improve you as he sees fit.

The Matthew 17 text on the previous page belongs to all of us as a living word. It is a valuable place to pray and meditate. It is the place when you ask God to make a moment with you—"I want to see Jesus in all his glory. I want the Holy Spirit to shine on me, and I want to hear your voice." What might your mountain experience look like? Let me give you some food for thought.

In Matthew 17:1–3, it says, "After six days Jesus took with him Peter, James and John the brother of James, and led them up a high mountain by themselves. There He was transfigured before them. His face shone like the sun, and His clothes became as white as the light. Just then there appeared before them Moses and Elijah, talking with Jesus." This has been their mountaintop experience. Don't look for their experience because something is designed just for you.

> Jesus entered Jericho and was passing through. A man was there by the name of Zacchaeus; he was a chief tax collector and was wealthy. He wanted to see who Jesus was, but because he was short, he could not see over the crowd. So, he ran ahead and climbed a sycamore-fig tree to see him, since Jesus was coming that way. When Jesus reached the spot, he looked up and said to him, "Zacchaeus, come down immediately. I must stay at your house today." So, he came down at once and welcomed him gladly. All the people saw this and began to mutter, "He has gone to be the guest of a sinner." But Zacchaeus stood up and said to the Lord, "Look, Lord! Here and now, I give half of my possessions to the poor, and if I have cheated anybody out of anything, I will pay back four times the amount." Jesus said to him, "Today salvation has come to this house, because this man, too, is a son of Abraham. For the Son of Man came to seek and to save the lost." (Luke 19:1–10)

Zacchaeus has felt he could not be any farther from God. His life in the world has been caught up into the devices of stealing and manipulating, and he has been dishonoring God to become a notable person in his society. The Roman authorities has also benefitted from his sin. These are the ways the world has destroyed the image of God in Zacchaeus, but Jesus has said, "Take heart, for I have overcome the world." When Zacchaeus climbs the tree to see the glory of Jesus, grace moves in his heart, and he meets the god he thought he will never see. Zacchaeus is transformed by the mountaintop Holy Spirit that shines like a new light on us all.

As I conclude this chapter, I am called to let you know that your life is already in the hands of God. You may think you are close to God or that you are far from God. Whatever the case is in your life, I encourage you to seek God. It is the best decision I have ever made. I hope and I pray for you all. Please choose eternal life with God the Father, the Son, and the Holy Spirit.

CHAPTER 5

The Opening

"Behold, I stand at the door and knock. If anyone hears My voice and opens the door, I will come into him and dine with him, and he with Me. To him who overcomes I will grant to sit with Me on My throne, as I also overcame and sat down with My Father on His throne. "He who has an ear, let him hear what the Spirit says to the churches." (Revelations 3:20–22 NKJV)

The text to start this chapter is a revelation of God through Christ Jesus to the disciple John. The church in that era longs to hear from God, and this is a new and welcomed communication from the Messiah that will meet that need. Therefore, the opening in the will of God is personal connection with all humanity and the individuals who listen faithfully are blessed.

It doesn't get any more personal than this. There is a quality of God's grace called prevenient grace. That is the grace of God that works in a person's life that causes them to seek or wonder about spirituality, eternal life, and the nature of God. Prevenient grace is the grace of God working before we are aware of it, which leads us to repent, seek, and learn more about God. Remember this is a gift from God. A person can be serious and even excited about God because that is how God's grace works. And then when the cares of the world surface, it can challenge the enthusiasm given to us by God the Holy Spirit.

> I will sprinkle clean water on you, and you will be clean; I will cleanse you from all your impurities and from all your idols. I will give you a new heart and put a new spirit in you; I will remove from you your heart of stone and give you a heart of flesh. And I will put my Spirit in you and move you to follow my decrees and be careful to keep my ways. (Ezekiel 36:25–28 NIV)

The important part to remember is that God is not looking for our permission. It is a matter of fact. "I will" in this text means it is put into motion already. There will be twists and turns on the road to eternal life and peace, and there will be times when you think you are alone.

I repeat, there will be twists and turns on the road to eternal life and peace, and there will times when you will think you are alone. You are never alone with God.

Hebrews 13:5 says, "Don't love money; be satisfied with what you have. For God has said, 'I will never fail you. I will never abandon you.'"

The text says, "Don't love money." It could really apply to anything in the world that takes all your attention and keeps you captive from enjoying your relationship with God and his people. There are times when work/career, education, and social position can call us away from our family and our family with God. The opening again is a heavenly union that is poured out upon us. Thousands of generations have experienced the opening of God's grace and have not known it, and if they have known it, some have rejected it. For many people, the opening occurs through Christ Jesus. They have learned the value and power of the opening of God's grace.

> When the people saw the thunder and lightning and heard the trumpet and saw the mountain in

> smoke, they trembled with fear. They stayed at a distance and said to Moses, "Speak to us yourself and we will listen. But do not have God speak to us or we will die." Moses said to the people, "Do not be afraid. God has come to test you, so that the fear of God will be with you to keep you from sinning." The people remained at a distance, while Moses approached the thick darkness where God was. Then the Lord said to Moses, "Tell the Israelites this: 'You have seen for yourselves that I have spoken to you from heaven: Do not make any gods to be alongside me; do not make for yourselves gods of silver or gods of gold." (Exodus 20:18–23)

Are you a person who has doubted the existence of God and the love of God and has chosen to make yourself or gold or silver as your god? If so, you are not alone.

Christ Jesus is God in the flesh. He has no doubts about his call or purpose as the second part of the Trinity. Although, he have had to deal with the chaos of the world he is saving. I remind you/me/us that we are not the messiah. God does not want us to be the messiah, but to be like Jesus in our fallen capacity. And that is the energy of the opening. God's grace and spirit is helping us. In the following verses, you will see the strength of Jesus and the weakness of his disciples.

> Jesus went out as usual to the Mount of Olives, and his disciples followed him. On reaching the place, he said to them, "Pray that you will not fall into temptation." He withdrew about a stone's throw beyond them, knelt down and prayed, "Father, if you are willing, take this cup from me; yet not my will, but yours be done." An angel from heaven appeared to him and strengthened him. And being in anguish, he prayed more ear-

nestly, and his sweat was like drops of blood falling to the ground. (Luke 22:39–44)

Now then, do you need the help of God to get through your ugly stuff? *Yes, you do!* The opening of God's grace to you/us comes with the power of the angels to support us. Jesus displays to the world that the omnipresence of God blankets his children. I want to remind us of all of our personal experiences in life and how they have become personal habits. Have you ever kicked the blankets off yourself? The circumstances of a person's life cause them to make decisions for their comfort's sake. Kicking the blanket of God's protection off your life is a dangerous idea. Yet people do it day in and day out to serve their personal desires.

During my years of jail ministry, most of the men were incarcerated on drug charges. Many of the men are involved with the production of meth. They will go to jail and get involved with the program I offered: to get out of their cell and have an hour or more of inspiration once a week. They often remark about how much better they feel. They will throw off the blanket.

They will throw off the blanket when they get released, often returning to the prior lifestyle. The spiritual protection they have had in the program has been kicked off, and their life has become a mess again. This does not just apply to jailed people. It applies to all people who find the grace of God in a transformed life. And sometimes, they find that they are trapped into previous lifestyles, and they throw off the protection of God's grace. I can leave this dialogue there and throw my hands up that "too many people are a lost cause." The only problem with that is, I know it is not the will of God. In the eyes of the Lord, there are no lost causes; that will assume that there is a limit to God's power.

The opening has many purposes. It starts the ball rolling toward a perception of God. It continues as a means of clarification of the truth and the role of God the Father, the Son, and the Holy Spirit for everyone. It opens the way for the closed and confused person. It opens the heart and soul to wonder and splendor. It opens us to the perfecting power of God on our body and soul. And that's what I intend to share now.

> Moses said to the Lord, "Pardon your servant, Lord. I have never been eloquent, neither in the past nor since you have spoken to your servant. I am slow of speech and tongue." The Lord said to him, "Who gave human beings their mouths? Who makes them deaf or mute? Who gives them sight or makes them blind? Is it not I, the Lord? Now go; I will help you speak and will teach you what to say." (Exodus 4:10–12)

Here is a typical response to God when we are scared and feel we cannot measure up to the call. Moses is called to a moment of service, and he feels very ill equipped. And I don't blame him. In this text, we are taught that God knows everything about our body and spirit, and He can make it work in ways we never imagined. God is the authority on his creation.

Moses becomes one of the most eloquent prophets of the Judaean and Christian faiths. Jesus heals the sick, and in John 9, Jesus restores the sight of a man born blind. Therefore, God in the days of Moses is the same God "who became flesh and dwelt among us in Christ Jesus" (John 1:14). Now what part of you is not understood by the mind of God?

In Luke 12: 6–7 (NIV), it says, "Jesus said, 'Are not five sparrows sold for two pennies? Yet not one of them is forgotten by God. And even the very hairs of your head are all numbered. So do not be afraid; you are worth more than many sparrows.'"

The same compassion and care revealed in the words of Jesus are present in the moment with Moses. God is the God who was, who is, and who is to come. And below, we read how God has arranged the circumstances of Moses's life to help him cope with the fears of his life. He has a plan to do the same with everyone.

> But Moses said, "Pardon your servant, Lord. Please send someone else. "Then the Lord's anger burned against Moses, and he said, "What about your brother, Aaron the Levite? I know he can speak well. He is already on his way to meet you, and he will be glad to see you. You shall speak to him and put words in his mouth; I will help both of you speak and will teach you what to do. He will speak to the people for you, and it will be as if he were your mouth and as if you were God to him." (Exodus 4:13–17)

I dare you to make a list of excuses and present them to God. I have tried that a couple of times. God is well aware of how Moses will respond. The text says, "The Lord's anger burned against Moses." This is a matter of fear versus faith. As much as God has been working to build Moses's faith, fear has been getting in the way. It will take a strategy on God's part to build faith in both Moses and Aaron, and it has worked. It always does, and that is God's grace at its best.

We have been discussing the opening of the heart and soul to the love, grace, and will of God. That event does not occur for no reason. The next part of "The Opening" is about what God intends to do with you, the child, the one he has opened to the his influence.

According to Max Lucado, "God loves you just the way you are, but he *refuses* to leave you that way. He wants you to be just like Jesus."

This will be exciting for some folks but hard to believe for others. This means that for the thirsty, rivers of living water will fill your heart, life, and soul. This is the place where the kingdom of God (heaven) is embraced and the place where it is rejected or ignored.

> Enter through the narrow gate. For wide is the gate and broad is the road that leads to destruction, and many enter through it. But small is the gate and narrow the road that leads to life, and only a few find it. (Matthew 7:13–14)

What do you think is Jesus talking about in this text? Commentaries and people of some faith say that it applies to the way to heaven. Hell is a wide path to destruction, and heaven is a very narrow path to eternal life. I certainly don't disagree with that thought process; although, it leaves out some really important spiritual details that the only the thirsty will understand.

"Wide is the path"—for the worldly nonbeliever or the limited believer, this is religious jargon. It absolutely is not that. I understand some religions have used Scripture to ridicule, manipulate, and even oppress people. And this is probably one of those Scriptures that can be used that way. But that is wrong. "The wide path" is what is revealed to us with very little substance. For instance, a used car salesman might say, "This is a great car—an older couple drove it to church every Sunday," and that's it. They do not give any details, and if you ask for their names, oh that is confidential information. The wide path does not guide you truthfully.

Have you ever had a friendship with someone who is part of the inside circle and they pull a few strings for you? I have a good friend. His name is Roger Carling. He has worked for a manufacturing company for a long time, even though we were not that far apart in age. I have needed a job while I was perusing my career in ministry.

Roger is a good employee and has a good reputation with his employer. He makes a recommendation to his employer to give me a job, and they do so. He pulls a few strings on my behalf. This is the narrow path in one sense. It is a relationship that makes your future have promise. I ask you, How many people have you known that are sincere and caring about your future? If you are truthful with yourself, the group narrows down quite quickly. Jesus is your messiah. That narrows the field immensely. The amazing part is that by focusing your faith on God and in Christ Jesus, you open yourself to a wide path of righteousness, spirituality, and eternal life. The narrow gate offers the widest opportunity to spiritual growth, expression, and love.

> Now Thomas (also known as Didymus), one of
> the Twelve, was not with the disciples when Jesus

> came. So, the other disciples told him, "We have seen the Lord!" But he said to them, "Unless I see the nail marks in his hands and put my finger where the nails were, and put my hand into his side, I will not believe." A week later his disciples were in the house again, and Thomas was with them. Though the doors were locked, Jesus came and stood among them and said, "Peace be with you!" Then he said to Thomas, "Put your finger here; see my hands. Reach out your hand and put it into my side. Stop doubting and believe." Thomas said to him, "My Lord and my God!" Then Jesus told him, "Because you have seen me, you have believed; blessed are those who have not seen and yet have believed." Thomas had decided to make the life gate very narrow due to his doubt and you see Jesus changed that. (John 20:24–29)

The opening is a place where God removes doubt and replaces it with faith. Thomas has experienced loss in his life prior to meeting Jesus. And in his relationship as a disciple, he has changed his mind about where God is. And we learn from the previous text that he is struggling again. Jesus has opened himself to Thomas, and that inspires him to let go of his past fears. And then the Messiah, the lord of his life, is now gone and gone in his mind to a terrible defeat. Therefore, when his fellow disciples said "We have seen the Lord," he scoffed.

What pain or struggle has caused you to say, "Where is God?"? Like many of us, you may have a list of things. While I was a hospice chaplain, I have met many people who believe God has never been or has left them. And we have to be sympathetic to those people in those heartbreaking moments. In Matthew 25:35–40 (NIV), it says, "Jesus said, 'I needed clothes, and you clothed me, I was sick, and you looked after me, I was in prison, and you came to visit me.' When did we see you sick or in prison and go to visit you?' The King will reply, 'Truly I tell you, whatever you did for one of the least of these brothers and sisters of mine, you did for me.'"

Thomas has needed a Lord who is willing to meet him in his moment of doubt and despair. Can you imagine the harassment the disciples took from the Jewish leaders and friends when Jesus has been crucified? Jesus has opened Thomas's heart and soul to the power of miracles and ministry. What that means is there is no replacement for the feeling of witnessing miracles and feeling a close and loving relationship. If you have ever felt abandoned by someone you love or who is very close to you, then you know the heart of Thomas. Jesus would not leave Thomas in that place of doubt and misery. And He will not leave you there either. What needs to be understood here is that Thomas has not left his fellowship. And every time we gather in faithful fellowship with Christians, Jesus is there.

When Jesus opens our heart and soul to the triune power of God, heaven and eternity reside within us. Thomas soon learns about that triune power, and when he has that intimate moment with Jesus, his response is this: "Thomas said to him, 'My Lord and my God!'" What is keeping you as a worldly bystander away from Jesus? Inside you is the same seed of faith and love that Thomas has tried to hide.

See how that worked out. You cannot ever say that I never knew Jesus. Maybe he came to you in the womb or maybe in other circumstances. Some call it déjà vu, something they already dreamed, but that is phony. You will believe it is Jesus if you, like Thomas, stay in the church, ministry, and fellowship. I am leading you to a fellowship of faith so that you may know Christ Jesus and know him to the fullest.

> When a Samaritan woman came to draw water, Jesus said to her, "Will you give me a drink?" (His disciples had gone into the town to buy food.) The Samaritan woman said to him, "You are a Jew, and I am a Samaritan woman. How can you ask me for a drink?" (For Jews do not associate with Samaritans.) Jesus answered her, "If you knew the gift of God and who it is that

asks you for a drink, you would have asked him, and he would have given you living water." "Sir," the woman said, "you have nothing to draw with and the well is deep. Where can you get this living water? 'Are you greater than our father Jacob, who gave us the well and drank from it himself, as did also his sons and his livestock?" "Jesus answered, "Everyone who drinks this water will be thirsty again, but whoever drinks the water I give them will never thirst. Indeed, the water I give them will become in them a spring of water welling up to eternal life." The woman said to him, "Sir, give me this water so that I won't get thirsty and have to keep coming here to draw water." (John 4:7–15)

Once you are opened to Jesus, everyone around you is changed also. The scripture of John 4, the Samaritan woman, is a perfect example of the power of the opening grace. The woman at the well has been doing the same things as every other day. That is the awesome part about God's grace. God knows your routines and looks for the opening.

In our current age of internet, Amazon, Facebook, and many other sites use cookies to track your searches, your purchases, your book, movie interests, and so on. By technology, they are able to track your activities online. Some people like it and are happy that they send you more stuff to research and purchase. And then some people think it is an invasion of their cyber privacy. (I don't believe there is such a thing as cyber privacy, oh well.)

God has been in the business of tracking your life steps, needs, and possibilities. He has been doing this for all his children, without cookies, and it is called grace. God is not interested in your most recent purchases as a holy salesman. God is interested in watching you accept the living water offered by Christ Jesus, which wells up into eternal life. Like the woman at the well, Jesus will meet you because he knows you are thirsty.

Jesus said, "Indeed, the water I give them will become in them a spring of water welling up to eternal life." The woman said to him, "Sir, give me this water so that I won't get thirsty and have to keep coming here to draw water." Many people would like to think this is a nice Bible story about a chance meeting between Jesus and the woman. That is not how the opening of the kingdom of God works. God in his triune nature is able to assess and process the lives of all his children. And this moment between Jesus and the Samaritan woman is the glory of God's grace at its best. This has been her day of salvation put in motion, which started when the Creator breathed life into her body while she was in her mother's womb.

I repeat, once you are opened to Jesus, everyone around you is changed also.

In John 4:25–26, "The woman said, 'I know that Messiah [called Christ] is coming. When he comes, he will explain everything to us.' Then Jesus declared, 'I, the one speaking to you—I am He.'" This woman has experienced grace at its best, opening her heart and soul. Her world experience has not been the best; she has lived somewhat of an indecent lifestyle. She comes to the well at a time when others would not, because she was shunned by her peers. To avoid conflict, she waits until all the other women are gone.

This is what God's grace is looking for and watching out for. She has been a lost sheep that needed to be brought back into the fold. This is the grace of God at work, monitoring your life and needs. Jesus and the woman meet, and it is not by accident. If you have met Jesus and received him as your personal savior, it has not been an accidental meeting. God has been looking for you. If you have not received Jesus as your personal savior, he will find you with a moment of grace, just when you need it. I know that Jesus is the Messiah, the son of the living God. I am ever grateful for my moment of grace. And if that were not enough, God has confirmed his grace in me by using me to help others see his grace.

> Many of the Samaritans from that town believed in Jesus because of the woman's testimony, "He told me everything I ever did." So, when the

Samaritans came to Him, they urged Him to stay with them, and He stayed two days. And because of His words many more became believers. They said to the woman, 'We no longer believe just because of what you said; now we have heard for ourselves, and we know that this man really is the Savior of the world." (John 4:39–42)

I and many other people have had these moments. When we dedicate our lives to following Jesus, the Holy Spirit takes over to work through us.

I want to share an incident in my life as a hospice chaplain here in southwest Florida that should assist in the idea of God taking over and working through us. I meet a man who is in his late sixties and has been diagnosed with less than six months to live. He has previously experienced surgery, chemotherapy, and radiation treating his cancer diagnosis and has enjoyed some success and remission. When I have met him, a few years has passed. His cancer comes back, and the treatment is too much for him. I call and schedule a meeting. He acknowledges himself as a Christian and says he has received Christ Jesus as his personal savior.

We talk for thirty minutes, and he says, "I will call you when I want you to come back again." We enjoy a moment of prayer and faith. The man has been married and has adult children. I call and stay in touch with the patient's wife and speak briefly with the patient on the phone for prayer.

Then one day, I get a call from an RN on the team, and she states that the man has passed away, and the family would like to see me before the undertaker arrived. Fortunately, I am only ten minutes away at the time. I arrive at the house to find the RN, the social worker, the wife still holding her husband who has passed away, and the family members milling about. I am welcomed by everyone, and the wife asks, "Can you do some kind of last rights prayer."

I say, "I can do more than that. I can give God glory for giving him to us and surrender him into the presence of God."

She says, "Please do."

After a special moment of worship, prayer, and surrendering the man to the kingdom of God, the family has felt better.

As I look around the house and the few rooms I can see, there are guitars and instruments nearby. I ask who plays guitar. The patient and all the family members are musicians. I say, "I play guitar. What kind of music did your husband like?" Southern Rock and Willy Nelson.

Continuing the work of God with family as a chaplain, I say, "I know some Willy Nelson songs. Should we play?" The patient's wife, son, and brother say that will be a perfect send-off to heaven. We play several songs, and our unity as musicians is amazing. The RN, the social worker, and the rest of the family are amazed. We play the man's favorite songs, and the son and brother feel they have honored their family. The family is so pleased, and the event is talked about for weeks to come. When we open ourselves to wisdom and insight of God, he uses the talents he has given us to change our lives and the lives of people around us. I am still in awe of God's all-knowing grace and power. Amen.

The last part of this chapter and the subject regarding the opening, I will focus on God opening our minds and spirits to the things to come. The apocalyptic (end-times) literature has been subject of fascination, controversy, and conflict for people for thousands of years, for both believers in God and nonbelievers. This is information shared by God sometimes through angels like Gabriel, through prophets (Daniel), through the Messiah in Christ Jesus, through the Holy Spirit, and through his faithful disciples, which could be you or me. The fascination with these scriptures has excited people into research and service, challenged people with fear, created fanaticism.

> While I, Daniel, was watching the vision and trying to understand it, there before me stood one who looked like a man. And I heard a man's voice from the Ulai calling, "Gabriel, tell this man the meaning of the vision." As he came near the place where I was standing, I was terrified and fell prostrate. "Son of man," he said to me,

"understand that the vision concerns the time of the end." While he was speaking to me, I was in a deep sleep, with my face to the ground. Then he touched me and raised me to my feet. (Daniel 8:15–18 NIV)

A vital point to understand here is that Daniel is flabbergasted and confused.

God knows that we will respond like Daniel to the glorious experiences of the kingdom of heaven and his angels. That in my mind is awesome, and I praise God that there is always another level of his grace and righteousness. These levels are to be experienced, and they are breathtaking. Daniel doesn't understand what he is seeing, and the angel Gabriel explains as much as he knows Daniel can understand. There are always going to be levels of God's holiness that will leave a person scratching their heads in wonder. With that in mind, I want you to remember there are millions of truths we can embrace in faith for our salvation and eternal life.

When you study the Book of Daniel, the first several chapters help the reader to learn about the God that Daniel has faith in—how he provides food, wisdom, and miracles to the dedicated believers. Then in the eight chapter, the reader begins to learn about the omnipresent nature of God. God purposely uses the book to take the reader on a journey of spiritual growth and awareness.

I remember learning how to play chess. I have thought they were figurines you could play castle games with, like cowboy and Indian figurines. Then I have learned the game is not like checkers. Then I have. learned the directions that each figure in the game could move, and then I have learned there were strategies to win, and I'm still working on those. Playing with the figurines like cowboys and Indians has only made me look foolish and naive. Although insight, wisdom, and sound strategies can make you a winner in chess and your spiritual life with God.

When a person approaches the books of Daniel or Revelation as a new believer or nonbeliever, they're likely to make foolish and naive assumptions about the message and character of God. Read the Gospels and the letters and get to know the character of God in Christ Jesus before you go to the last chapter, revealing the most glorious part of God's nature. I have studied these books for years, and there is always something new and exciting to learn.

> And afterward, I will pour out my Spirit on all people. Your sons and daughters will prophesy, your old men will dream dreams, your young men will see visions. Even on my servants, both men and women, I will pour out my Spirit in those days. I will show wonders in the heavens and on the earth. (Joel 2:28–30)

This Old Testament text is the word of God through a prophet named Joel. He shares with the reader that God intends his children to have amazing spiritual experiences. They will dream dreams and see visions of the great and glorious kingdom of God and his holiness. This is intended to let the reader/follower/believer know there is more to meet the eyes of the believer.

This leads me to a subject that needs to be clarified. There are people in our culture who have been around for thousands of years calling themselves seers, physics, sorcerers, and any other title they use. Many of them claim to have visions and information about the spiritual realm. It is important to peruse this area very carefully. It is an arena of angels and demons, and the only one in charge of this arena is Christ Jesus. I have heard and watched physics make claims that are for the purpose of income and addiction to their spiritual environments. They lead people into very dangerous and unprotected spiritual areas.

I have once attended a physic conference in New York. It has been a weekend event. There are people calling themselves reverend, despite not having degrees from a seminary and no experience in the area of spiritual awareness with God the Father, the Son, and the Holy Spirit. I have spent several hours there to learn about this area of spiritualism, and I have left very concerned and dirty. I am concerned for the souls of the people because evil is being summoned, and I feel dirty because I know the cleansing power of Christ Jesus. This is an area of darkness in many circumstances. When you open your soul to any realm outside of Christ Jesus, you may be destroyed.

The opening is both exciting and fearful. With Jesus and the Holy Spirit guiding you, you are protected from the evil one (the devil). Without Jesus and the Holy Spirit, you are at risk for spiritual disaster.

I will share a real experience in a hospital as a chaplain. In this hospital, there are two chaplains, one Roman Catholic for all the Catholic patients and one Protestant for all the Protestant patients, Jews, Muslims, Buddhists, and nonbelievers, and that is me. I meet a man who requests a chaplain visit, and he is not a churchgoer and has been a believer through his life experiences.

I meet the man, and he is tied to the bed thrashing uncontrollably. The RN is giving him seizure medication as much as directed and is possible to give. The medication has provided little or no relief to the patient. The man can talk, and when I told him I was the chaplain, he said, "Pray for me." I pray for him, and I tell him I will be back to check on him. I return to find him in the same miserable condition. I speak with him, and again, I pray for the man. It seems that in those moments of prayer, there is some subsiding of the convulsions. Later that night, I pray about the man in my personal prayer time and ask God for guidance. The Holy Spirit says, "Cast the demon out of him."

I am alarmed and has never considered doing such a thing in public. I have thought, *Those people will think I'm an idiot or fanatic.* But God does not let it go from my mind. The next day, I go to the patient who is the same. I say, "God has told me to cast this demon out of you as far as the east is from the west," and I prayed. The man shrieks, and it is horrible to watch. The RN runs in, and I have thought, *What have I done?* I leave to let the staff attend to him. The next day, when I arrived at the hospital, he is sitting up and eating. He said, "Thank you for not giving up."

This story reveals to us the precarious nature of the spiritual arena. Without sound and solid faith teaching about the nature and character of God the Father, the Son, and the Holy Spirit, we will have struggles and possible destruction to both body and spirit.

> After this I looked, and there before me was a great multitude that no one could count, from every nation, tribe, people, and language, standing before the throne and before the Lamb. They were wearing white robes and were holding palm branches in their hands. And they cried out in a loud voice: "Salvation belongs to our God, who sits on the throne, and to the Lamb." (Revelations 7:9–10 NIV)

This above text is a witness to the protective and eternal power of God in Christ Jesus. You can take a lot of time trying to discern who the multitude is and what tribe or people, and you will be missing the point. The multitude are people who believe in Christ Jesus and learn about his character. Some religions people and leaders debate this stuff, and that reveals their naivete.

> Then one of the elders asked me, "These in white robes—who are they, and where did they come from?" I answered, "Sir, you know."
> And he said, "These are they who have come out of the great tribulation; they have washed their robes and made them white in the blood of the Lamb. Never again will they hunger; never again will they thirst. The sun will not beat down on them, nor any scorching heat. For the Lamb at the center of the throne will be their shepherd; 'he will lead them to springs of living water." And God will wipe away every tear from their eyes." (Revelations 7:13–17 NIV)

Friends, brothers, and sisters, we cannot travel this spiritual journey with a risky, nonchalant attitude. With Christ Jesus, I have enjoyed some of the most intimate spiritual experiences with him and those who have gone before me. Amen.

I am closing the chapter with a couple of Scriptures from the letter to the Jews who are converts to Jesus and the Gospel. The author/authors do not reveal themselves. Some commentators believe it was the apostle Paul and his coworkers in the faith. The letter is to help the people stay focused on God as they experience the challenges of the world.

I want to meet you in this moment, wherever you are in your God/faith journey. Is the opening the new opportunity of finding out that there really is a God who created all things, including you? Then I encourage you to bask in your new relationship with God the Father, the Son, and the Holy Spirit. Get in a good Bible-teaching church, where you can hear the rich truths of how much God loves you. Let fellowship and worship light a fire in your soul and help quench your spiritual thirst.

If you have been in the church as a fan and not really a participant, then I tell you, you don't know what you are missing. You are created to go onto perfection and to enjoy the journey. You will feel the influence of the cloud of witnesses and the angels you think are strangers.

To you folks who have been in this relationship for a long time, you are the ones Christ Jesus is counting on to be the opening to others for him.

> Therefore, since we are surrounded by such a great cloud of witnesses, let us throw off everything that hinders and the sin that so easily entangles. And let us run with perseverance the race marked out for us, fixing our eyes on Jesus, the pioneer and perfecter of faith. (Hebrews 12:1–2)

> Keep on loving one another as brothers and sisters. Do not forget to show hospitality to strangers, for by so doing some people have shown hospitality to angels without knowing it. (Hebrews 13:1–2)

CHAPTER 6

Where Am I?

The next day John the Baptist was there again with two of his disciples. When he saw Jesus passing by, he said, "Look, the Lamb of God!" When the two disciples heard him say this, they followed Jesus. Turning around, Jesus saw them following and asked, "What do you want?" They said, "Rabbi" (which means "Teacher"), "where are you staying?" Come," He replied, "and you will see." So, they went and saw where He was staying, and they spent that day with him. It was about four in the afternoon. (John 1:35–39 NKJV)

This chapter is intended to help the reader to know thyself. A lot of people want to leave this arena a mystery even to themselves. The above scripture is about two disciples who are looking for peace in their soul amidst the unsettledness of the world. When these two disciples of John the Baptist hear him say, "Look, the Lamb of God!" They follow Jesus because they are looking for the next direction for their lives with God.

These two men become John's disciples when they hear him proclaim, "I offer you a baptism of repentance for the forgiveness of sins." They are baptized, and they follow him. As John the Baptist states," I am not the Messiah. I come to prepare the way for Him." John feels a responsibility to lead his disciples to Jesus, the one who can do more for them than he can do and more than they ever imagined. These two disciples are enjoying a new spiritual life experience. And then there is the moment when they realize in their minds that Jesus ultimately answers their soul's question, Where Am I?

Throughout this chapter, you will be encouraged and challenged to answer that question, Where am I? The purpose is to get real with yourself about what makes you tick. Are you completely focused on achievement? I have been there—take it from a person who worked to get a doctor of divinity degree. Why am I doing what I am doing?

Sometimes we can get so caught up into achieving certain goals that we lose ourselves, our awareness, and our direction. The reason I feel this is so important is due to the hundreds of people I meet as a chaplain who feel like lost sheep during their times of struggle and end of life. Trust me, you do not want to come to a place of redirection or end without any information about God the Father, the Son, and the Holy Spirit and your eternal circumstances. I have walked through those arenas of panic and dismay with more people than I care to remember.

Just like in the John 1 text, there is something missing in the disciples lives, and the appeal of Jesus is calling them. Many of the patients I meet have had some background experience with religion. Some are Jews, some Christians, some Muslim, some Buddhist, and some Hindu or a mixture of all. More times than none, these people have a limited understanding of their religious titles and very limited experience or participation in their religion of choice. At the end of life, the "Where am I?" question really becomes an important question to answer for spiritual and internal peace.

Psalm 121:1–2 (NLT) says, "I lift up my eyes to the mountains—where does my help come from? My help comes from the Lord, the Maker of heaven and earth." The psalmist is looking beyond himself for the support and presence of the Lord. Why do people do that?

Worldly success and power provide a limited sense of comfort and peace. The COVID-19 movement that has swept across our society has forced people into looking for new jobs and sources of income. Some of the sources come in the form of unemployment and subsidized income. The only problem is that the world and many local governments do not function under the eternal premise. In other words, it's a quick fix. Just when you feel secure, the world commitment to you ends.

The psalmist says, "I lift up my eyes to the mountains."

"Come," Jesus replies, "and you will see." Jesus says to his followers, "Come and you will see." This is about is the power of Jesus that is aware of your life circumstances. The psalmist knows in his heart there is something greater than him to seek. It is about the power of God living in Jesus. Jesus knows more about what those disciples want and need than they know themselves. The same is still happening today. God never stops asking me, Where are you?

Genesis 3:8–9 says, "Then the man and his wife heard the sound of the Lord God as He was walking in the garden in the cool of the day, and they hid from the Lord God among the trees of the garden. But the Lord God called to the man, 'Where are you?'" They have convinced themselves they can hide from God, but that doesn't happen.

We need to know that God is talking to each one of us when he asks, "Where are you?" This is a question that is relevant to all our current circumstances. Like Adam and Eve's situation, the Lord has never taken his eyes off from them. He has a plan for how he wants matters to turn out. I have tried to hide matters in my heart and soul, thinking God will not see my sins. Not going to happen. I have learned to confess my sins and ask God to forgive me and lead me to understand more about where I am in my life journey and relationship with God and his people.

> Very truly I tell you, whoever hears My word and believes Him who sent me has eternal life and will not be judged but has crossed over from death to life. Very truly I tell you, a time is coming and

has now come when the dead will hear the voice of the Son of God and those who hear will live. For as the Father has life in himself, so he has granted the Son also to have life in himself. And he has given him authority to judge because He is the Son of Man.(John 5:24–27 NIV)

The previous scripture reveals a principle that God is managing where we are. Jesus says believing in God has an influence over our life circumstances that we can't control. As a believer, I have crossed over from death to life. Humor me for a moment. If I have controlled my eternal circumstances by only believing in God but doing what I want to, I am fooling myself. Faith and believing in God require interaction with God. I believe the sun and moon exist because I have spent time looking and studying them. I believe bald eagles can catch fish because I have spent time watching them. When a person believes in the power of God in their life, it is due to the fact that there is a relationship with God through the power of the Holy Spirit.

There have been many times when I feel inspired to read a certain scripture or reach out to a Christian friend for fellowship or to support them. The scripture would be exactly what I needed to hear, and the friend will say, "How did you know I needed your support?" I realize it is God interacting with me for my own needs and for those around me. When I have become a new Christian, I wake up one morning with the words in my mind, "God, I long for you." I thought, *I don't usually talk like that or use those words.* I pick up my Bible and just open it in a random spot. I open Psalm 63.

> O God, You *are* my God; Early will I seek You; My soul thirsts for You; My flesh longs for You In a dry and thirsty land Where there is no water. So, I have looked for You in the sanctuary, to see Your Power and Your glory. (Psalms 63:1–2 NKJV; italics added)

REV. RICHARD STACKHOUSE

When I read the words of Psalm 63, I am awestruck. I have heard from the Lord. God has chosen to reveal how he watches over me both day and night, and he also wants to show me what it means to be led in the path of righteousness. Since then, I guess cause I listened, I have heard from God many times.

> Jesus said, "Do not be amazed at this, for a time is coming when all who are in their graves will hear His voice and come out—those who have done what is good will rise to live, and those who have done what is evil will rise to be condemned. By myself I can do nothing; I judge only as I hear, and my judgment is just, for I seek not to please myself but Him who sent me." (John 5:28–30)

I share this scripture because it is inspired by God for us to know that people are in vastly different stages and places in their spiritual journey. God is merciful, mighty, and the true master of comfort and peace. Many people have had religious and church experiences that turn them against the idea of God. The truth is that God knows that and is working to heal those hurtful feelings. What this text is about are the social environments and the impact they have on a child of God. If corruption is an area that a person enjoys and they thrive on hurting and manipulating other people that belong to God, then evil has overtaken them, and they have resigned themselves to eternal condemnation.

On the other hand, there are those people who have the character to live by doing for others as they would want others to do for them. They have done what is good. Unless a person lives in a bubble, a monastery, or the kingdom of God, we are going to experience examples of good and evil. We need to ask ourselves, Where am I in all this?

During my years of jail ministry, I have met many people who have not learned to determine where they fit in to their environment and which side of good and evil to embrace. Many of them are men I have really grown to like, and they like me too. More times than

I like to realize, men say to me, "This is the only place where I am clean and sober." People need to accept what moves them to enjoy a meaningful and good life. Ask yourselves, "Where am I?"

I don't need you all to call or email me to tell me where you are; although I am a recognized spiritual counselor, and I like to help people. My contact information is provided if that is your desire. I have also met many Christians who have belonged to churches for a long time, but they are not sure where they are in the whole scheme of things between good and evil.

Some people function under the premise of fear. They are afraid they are going to do something to mess it all up—in other words, screw up and go to hell. As a pastor, they are tough to be around and also to convince that they are saved by God's grace and not their own actions. Grace shapes our actions into something better than we can do alone. Fear can be crippling for people, and it can become a tool of the hand of the devil.

I would like to share an incident that I have experienced as a chaplain with a few people of different life environments than mine and yet how God's grace managed the circumstances. I meet a lady who is dying from metastatic breast cancer. She lives for about six more weeks. She is a lesbian, and her partner is staying by her side. Everyone who moves through these precious moments of transition feels something from God, and many people don't know what to do, say, or feel in these moments. Meeting them as a chaplain and learning about the patient's spiritual concerns, I know God is helping her through this transition time.

What I have to managed is their fears, prejudices, and grief. The first thing that has been established is that the grace of God in Christ Jesus is for the whole world. When they all realize that heaven is the important matter at hand, quickly the grace of God starts building relationship and an understanding of a new life in heaven. We all become more aware that we are children of God. The patient becomes comfortable and peaceful.

Every person starts to learn more about their "where I am." I walk into the patient's room, and they greet me with excitement, because we all learn to put aside the agenda of life and world descriptions to realize faith in God the Father, the Son, and the Holy Spirit is the mightier than division. We hug, we laugh, we cry, and we pray; and the patient passes into the peace that passes all understanding. I pray that whoever reads these words that they do not try to redefine this author's commitment to the Bible and evangelical service. It is because of this author's commitment to the Bible, like the Apostle Paul, that "I have learned to be all things to all people in need of the love of Christ Jesus."

> So, Naomi and Ruth traveled until they came to Bethlehem. When they entered Bethlehem, the whole city was stirred because of them, and the women of the city exclaimed, "Can this be Naomi?" Do not call me Naomi," she replied. "Call me Mara because the Almighty has dealt quite bitterly with me. I went away full, but the Lord has brought me back empty. Why call me Naomi? After all, the Lord has testified against me, and the Almighty has afflicted me." So, Naomi returned from the land of Moab with her daughter-in-law Ruth the Moabitess. And they arrived in Bethlehem at the beginning of the barley harvest. (Ruth 1:19–22)

The Old Testament text above is one about the despair of a faithful woman and her family. Her struggle is with the "Why me, Lord?" question. I feel this is a necessary conversation for all of us who have had struggles in the past and still feels challenged and possibly that God is punishing us. Some people have asked me during these life struggles, "Is God getting even with me for something?" I remind them of the righteousness nature of God. I have said numerous times, if God were a "get even" god, he would have gotten even with me a long time ago. I have given Him plenty of reasons to.

In the Old Testament book of Ruth, when Naomi and Ruth are returning to Bethlehem, the women recognize her and call her by name. She says, "Do not call me Naomi." She replies, "Call me

Mara because the Almighty has dealt quite bitterly with me. I went away full, but the Lord has brought me back empty." Naomi and her husband leaves Bethlehem and goes to Moab because there is famine in Israel.

It would have been her husband's decision to take her and his sons to Moab. That is the customs of the era. Naomi still feels that God has caused her suffering in Moab. The reality is that her husband and sons are not hearty men, and in a place where there are some provisions but limited at best, they die. It is not unreasonable for Naomi to feel the way she does. And in the same way, when people suffer, they ask, "What have I done to deserve this?" Naomi, in her despair, also knows life with God has possibilities, and she continues to remember their customs and share them with Ruth. And moment by moment, God reinvents their life circumstances with abundant provisions and redemption. The world may challenge us, but it is important to remember what God says: "Today I do something new." Redemption is always the plan of God for believers and his children.

> The word of the Lord came to Jonah son of Amittai, "Go to the great city of Nineveh and preach against it, because its wickedness has come up before Me." But Jonah ran away from the Lord and headed for Tarshish. He went down to Joppa, where he found a ship bound for that port. After paying the fare, he went aboard and sailed for Tarshish to flee from the Lord. (Jonah 1:1–3)

This is a familiar story for many people, especially believers and churchgoers. Some people know they are running from the Lord. And then there are as many, or maybe even more, people who don't realize they are running away from the lure of God.

The first chapter reveals God's quest for you and the world. Jonah is a prophet of God; he has been a religious person, and he has run away from God. Have you ever said to yourself or someone else,

"I'm not a religious person"? To the hundreds of people that have said that to me in order to remove themselves from any type of religious conversation or a belief in God, are you here? I have listened to people talk about their life experiences, and so many times, they share an incident that can only be described as godly. And in those moments, they learn where they are and more about where they are going in this stage of life and in the time to come.

Jonah is not willing to admit where he is in his own emotional and spiritual life. In his life story, the people God has sent him to are evil and disrespectful to God and other faith people. Jonah has his own fears and prejudices that causes him to ignore and run from God. And his response to facing his problems is to run away. The following scripture tells us how that has worked out.

> The sea was getting rougher and rougher. So, they asked him, "What should we do to you to make the sea calm down for us?" "Pick me up and throw me into the sea," he replied, "and it will become calm. I know that it is my fault that this great storm has come upon you." (Jonah 1:11–12)

Jonah's life gets rougher and chaotic as he tries to deny his doubts and fears. He actually says to the men on the ship to throw him overboard; he would rather drown than face his fears.

I have had a man say to me once, "I have been bad all my life, so I know I am going to hell, and I won't see Jesus." I remind him of John 5: 28–29, where Jesus says, "Do not be amazed at this, for a time is coming when all who are in their graves will hear his voice and come out—those who have done what is good will rise to live, and those who have done what is evil will rise to be condemned." We meet Jesus either way, on the way to heaven or hell. He says, "I suppose I should decide which way I will see Him."

I say, "He came here to give you life eternal."

Just when this friend of mine has imagined his destiny is hell, God has done something new. The man starts going to church with his wife and receives the relationship charted out for him from the beginning of time.

Jonah 1: 17 says, "Now the Lord provided a huge fish to swallow Jonah, and Jonah was in the belly of the fish three days and three nights." This scripture is to teach you that whatever it takes to connect, reconnect, and remind you of the love of God, God will do it. I once have had a man, a member of the church, who is a trucker. He says that he has some questions about God and faith, and he asks me if I am willing to talk about it as we drive over the road. I agree, and we spend about thirty-six hours together in his truck. After twenty-four hours with me in the cab, I'm sure he would have rather been swallowed by the large fish. By the time we return home, he has dealt with a lot of past issues, family issues, and doubts and fears. It has been a good learning time for me as well. He has become more faith-centered and attended church regularly. He has never asked me to go over the road with him again. He has found a holy copilot.

> I am not saying this because I am in need, for I have learned to be content whatever the circumstances. I know what it is to be in need, and I know what it is to have plenty. I have learned the secret of being content in any and every situation, whether well fed or hungry, whether living in plenty or in want. I can do all this through him who gives me strength. (Philippians 4:11–13 NIV)

The Scripture above is a letter the Apostle Paul sent to the church in Philippi. These are the words of man who has spent all his life in religion and religious study. He is a Pharisee in the Jewish Sanhedrin, and then he meets the Lord and spends the rest of his life following Jesus.

The Apostle Paul says, "I have learned the secret of being content in any and every situation, whether well fed or hungry, whether living in plenty or in want." This is about developing a disciplined attitude in our emotions, our minds, and our spirits. These are areas of our person that are more difficult to direct than our bodies. Athletes develop training programs for their bodies that allow them to accomplish amazing skills for their given sport. Yet when an injury or defeat occurs, we may see that their emotion, mind, and spirit are not as well-trained as their bodies.

Fanny Crosby

Frances Jane Crosby was born on March 24, 1820, in the village of Brewster, about 50 miles north of New York City. She was the only child of John Crosby and his second wife Mercy Crosby. At six weeks old, Crosby caught a cold and developed inflammation of the eyes, mustard poultice was applied to treat the discharges. According to Crosby, this procedure damaged her optic nerves and blinded her, but modern physicians think that her blindness was more likely congenital and, given her age, may simply not have been noticed by her parents.

In this atmosphere of darkness and gloom, Fanny became increasingly introspective over her soul's welfare. She began to realize that something was lacking in her spiritual life. She knew that she had gotten wrapped up in social, political, and educational reform, and did not have a true love for God in her heart. She was, however, a fellow traveler of the Wesleyan holiness movement, including prominent members of the American Holiness movement in her circle of friends and attending Wesleyan/Holiness camp meetings.

Fanny Cosby was searching for spiritual fulfillment; she was in that place of personal and emotionally and physical challenges and in this quandary. Where am I? She asked God and then she found peace with God. This is the ultimate "where am I" environment. We all get here the important part is getting through this.

For example, she was a friend of Walter and Phoebe Palmer, "the mother of the holiness movement" and "arguably the most influential female theologian in Christian history," and their daughter Phoebe Knapp, with whom she wrote "Blessed Assurance"; she often visited the Methodist camp grounds at Ocean City, NJ as their guest. ("Franny Crosby," Wikipedia.com)

We all get here, in one way or another, that the important part is getting through this. I use this devoted lady as an example of real-life people who accept their circumstances whatever they are.

I redirect our thoughts to the words of the Apostle Paul of contentment in all circumstances. The Apostle Paul and the amazing Christian and hymn writer Fanny Cosby have learned to rise above their current circumstances and embrace the strength, love, and peace of God for perseverance. The vital lesson we learn from both people is their faith and commitment to the gospel of Christ Jesus. Our redemption and eternal strength are found in Christ Jesus our Lord. The Apostle Paul says, "I can do all this through him who gives me strength."

Where am I? There comes a time in all our lives when this question has everything to do with what we have lived through in our past, what we have argued with God about, and what we have accomplished because of all those experiences. A person of faith eventually sees this as a journey with God and his love for them. A nonbeliever sees this as some kind of karma.

What have I done in this world to cause it to get even with me? And usually, that is a never-ending list of past issues, lies, and regrets. The worldly corruptions do play games with the emotions of peoples, but God does not. In a relationship with God, we learn truthfully "where I am." These stories and scriptures are examples of mighty religious leaders, the jailed, the sick, or the trucker. Just ask God "Where am I?" and he will come to help you see your way through.

"Where am I?" can be transformed to "where I am" with the help of God and personal commitment. Some of us, like the Apostle Paul and Fanny Cosby, we have asked the question "Where am I?" in this unpredictable environment called life. God says, "I will never leave you, nor forsake you." It requires from both Paul and Fanny a commitment to learn about the power of God and to be willing to let the power of God function in them through the Holy Spirit.

We will always be asking the big questions like "Where am I?" in the plan of God, and we will learn that the answer to this question is the result of our limited insight. Don't lose hope. We have the opportunity to enjoy a relationship with God the Father, the Son, and the Holy Spirit where unlimited love, wisdom, and insight will be share with us as needed. I close this chapter with these words of the psalmist who has experienced his share of ups and downs and all the time God has been there.

> I lift up my eyes to the mountains—where does my help come from?
> My help comes from the Lord, the Maker of heaven and earth.
> He will not let your foot slip—he who watches over you will not slumber.
> Indeed, he who watches over Israel will neither slumber nor sleep.
> The Lord watches over you—the Lord is your shade at your right hand.
> The sun will not harm you by day, nor the moon by night.
> The Lord will keep you from all harm—he will watch over your life;
> The Lord will watch over your coming and going both now and forevermore. (Psalm 121:1–8 NIV)

CHAPTER 7

Who Am I?

Then God said, "Let us make human beings in our image, to be like us. They will reign over the fish in the sea, the birds in the sky, the livestock, all the wild animals on the earth, and the small animals that scurry along the ground." So, God created human beings in his own image. In the image of God, He created them; male and female he created them. Then God blessed them and said, "Be fruitful and multiply. Fill the earth and govern it. Reign over the fish in the sea, the birds in the sky, and all the animals that scurry along the ground." (Genesis 1:26–28 NLT)

I am starting this chapter called "Who Am I?" with the facts of our existence before any human has been aware of it. For thousands of years, human societies look for the answers to our existence. In the process of humans trying to explain their own lives, debates and research have led to false beliefs and definitions of religions and wars over those beliefs and definitions. Therefore, as people continue to function as the careless beings, then peace and societies will suffer.

God watches with holy influence and grace for millions of years over all that is created. Many societies feel the influence and misunderstands it and, in some ways, rejects God's disciplined influence. God knows the debate that would arise once he introduces himself to humanity. Consequently, he puts off the introduction for as long as he feels necessary. If we can now do some self-reflecting, it is easier and more appealing to do everything selfishly—"It's all about me." The selfless influences that come from God don't always match my desires and agenda.

Ecclesiastes 3:10–11 says, "I have seen the burden God has laid on the human race. He has made everything beautiful in its time. He has also set eternity in the human heart; yet no one can fathom what God has done from beginning to end." These words of King Solomon are the by-product of his own self-reflection. Everyone comes to a place of self-reflection eventually.

The challenge is what direction a person moves forward in and what philosophies the person listens to and possibly accepts. Jews, Christians, and Muslims all believe in one god. For the Jews and Muslims, it is the god of Abraham, Isaac, and Jacob; and for Christians, it is the same including Christ Jesus as the messiah, the son of the Living God. For Buddhists, Hindus, and many other religions, there are philosophies of many gods, no gods, and on and on.

The important point to consider is, many people have a skewed image of God, and they also have a skewed self-image. When a person accepts that they are created in the image of God, then their self-image is precious. "Let us make human beings in our image, to be like us." A look into the art for centuries that try to depict the image of God and the company of heaven, some of the images are beautiful, some are ominous, and some are outrageous. The one image that really seems to inspire some people, challenge some people, and create debate is the image of Christ Jesus. He is the son of the Living God, the god in the flesh recorded in the gospel of John.

John 1: 14 says, "God became flesh and dwelt among us." That is John's firsthand knowledge of Christ Jesus.

The author of this text will, at times, rest his head on the shoulder of Jesus. It is through this personal relationship with Christ Jesus that the disciple of John is able to get a better picture of his own value and self-image. People will know their own value when they get a close as they can to Christ Jesus. And now that Jesus sits at the right hand of God in the kingdom of heaven, he can do his ministry in a wider range, with power of the Holy Spirit. All people can now lie their head on the shoulder of Christ Jesus with the uniting presence of the Holy Spirit, and their image is restored to its original beauty.

Now comes the gift of faith. God gives a measure of faith to everyone. Like any valuable gift, it requires using it. In order to use faith, we need to be willing to walk into those places where faith is used and required. What that means is to act and decide that even if we don't have the answer, we will go where Jesus leads. Jesus has called the apostle Paul to follow him in a new direction. Paul knows this is his new calling from God, and he responds by faith, not knowing where it would eventually lead him.

The Apostle Paul writes in a letter to the church in Galatia, "I have been crucified with Christ and I no longer live, but Christ lives in me. The life I now live in the body, I live by faith in the Son of God, who loved me and gave himself for me" (Galatians 2:20).

Faith opens the door to possibilities that usually are not considered. For example, my personal spiritual connection with God the Father, the Son, and the Holy Spirit has occurred during the reading of the gospel according to John 15:5. "Jesus said, 'I am the Vine, you are the branches. If I am in you and you are in me, you will bear much fruit. But without me you can do nothing.'" What that means to me is that Jesus has included me into his life and purpose. Who am I? From that very moment, I am a branch of Jesus—meaning, my image has changed from me alone to me in the arena where my created image is being restored by the power and grace of God.

I don't know where this relationship change will lead. With some apprehension, my faith and trust in God overpower my fears, and I have decided I am going where he will take me. And this means me leaving New York State, where I have grown up and all my family lives. It has also helped me to trust more in the guidance of God; there is no family net to fall back on. I am being educated for pastoral ministry. This puts me in a social arena where I meet some really smart, supportive, and devout people.

Consequently, these people has helped to build my faith in the process God uses as he equips the called. I have spent almost four years in Bible college earning a bachelor's degree in religions and religious practices. I have learned to discipline myself for studies and also spiritual and character development. Part of my past life is like many people—not always making good decisions and experiencing a divorce. Many colleges and religious denominations do not accept people who have been divorced. And for some people, their past decisions are bad enough to ever get arrested or charged with some type of crime. Fortunately, that has never been my experience.

I have been supplied with a mentor who was a professor at a religious school. He has been graciously stern. His name is Rev. Stone. He wants to learn what type of personal character I have—was I honest, hardworking, and growing in my faith in God the Father, the Son, and the Holy Spirit?

He appreciates that my grades have been As and B+s. He also set me up for some unexpected events (unexpected to me, that was) to see how I will handle the given situation. These events consist of different types, such as leading worship in a church where the pastor is gone for a week or two, going to a hospital to visit people I have never met, and going to a home of people who have not been in church for a long time.

The preaching part has always worked out well. I am nervous enough to be extra prepared. The part of being compassionate to people when they suffered is a growth area for me. I certainly have the compassion for their circumstances, but I have been concerned with saying the right thing. It turns out that sincere compassion has an extraordinary language, even in the silence. And visiting the people who have not been in church for a long time was also a learning curve. I have to be encouraging more than judgmental. Elvis Presley sang a song "Walk a Mile in My Shoes." There is a line that goes, "Before you abuse, criticize, or accuse, walk a mile in my shoes."

Everyone has a mile or two of life experiences that influence their decisions. And with the people who have not been going to church, I learn that one lost his job and couldn't afford to put any money in the offering envelope. So he decided not to go to church. I told him to write a Bible verse from the New Testament and put it in the envelope and come to church, and the money will come eventually. Within one month after returning to church and offering Bible verses, the man has been offered a better job than he had before, including higher pay. God is always with us.

> Let love and faithfulness never leave you; bind them around your neck, write them on the tablet of your heart. Then you will win favor and a good name in the sight of God and man. Trust in the Lord with all your heart and lean not on your own understanding; in all your ways submit to Him, and He will make your paths straight. (Proverbs 3:3–6 NIV)

Each one of these experiences has provided me the chance to learn more about who I am now and that God has a converting role in my life. It is the will of God to improve our image moment by moment until we see him again face-to-face. One of the reasons I love being a Christian is the fellowship and inspiration. I have been with very healthy churches and church families, and I have experienced friendship, love, and learning more about God and his people. Healthy environments promote healthy people.

In these healthy church experiences, I realize I am learning more about the Bible and start memorizing some verses. For instance, this verse from the twenty-seventh chapter of the Old Testament book of Proverbs is another way God is shaping my life.

In Proverbs 27:17 (NLT), it says, "As iron sharpens iron, so a friend sharpens a friend." I have always had a friend who studies with me and has been committed in keeping each other accountable of learning about Jesus and following his examples of love and righteousness.

There is important subject to consider in the role of friendship and accountability partners, and that subject is graciousness. I have known people who have entered into these roles, and they become judgmental and critical of each other. Nothing stifles personal and spiritual growth faster than inconsiderate criticism. It is important to enter into these types of roles with people of similar values and personality traits. These types of roles and relationships require compassion and kindness because many of us experience similar challenges in this life journey, and we need to support and encourage one another.

As a chaplain, I have met and counseled many people in their medical and spiritual challenges, and that is *not* the time to become an accountability partner to someone. The obvious reason is that you are not in the same life circumstances. Often, people of faith think that their chaplain will do something like that. Remember, the person who is in the crisis moment cannot reciprocate mutual support as an accountability partner.

I want to share an experience I have had with a patient. I will call him Jonah. He is in the midforties age group and a longtime Christian. His father is an assistant chaplain for a retirement community, and faith in God is part of his life. Jonah is an addict. He is addicted to alcohol, oxycodone, and a number of other drugs. He lives with his parents, and they are out of their league with how to handle their son. The patient and I develop a close faith friendship, and we pray together often. Jonah has resigned to the fact that his addictions will kill him.

His parents, on the other hand, are grasping at straws to find someone or something that will heal their son of his issues. Because Jonah and I have a good relationship, he does have times of productive sobriety. He will read the Bible, and at one point, he becomes clean and finds a job. But when he is challenged, his response is to return to drugs and alcohol. I will get a call that Jonah is near death in the hospital after a binge of drugs and alcohol.

A year and a half later, Jonah dies of drug and alcohol poisoning. Jonah has been a man of faith. He has loved gospel music and Jesus. And yet he is frozen in the looking-backward syndrome. I know Jesus loves Jonah and, in death, he is released from his prison. Jonah's eternal circumstances are in the hands of Jesus. I spend several months with his parents after Jonah's death.

I mention this for the sake of the people who want to do support ministries as an extension of their churches outreach, such as Stephen's Ministries. Don't get it over your heads, and make sure you have the training needed and to learn how to set boundaries.

One more area in people's lives that have the opportunity of accountability is the relationship between the husband and wife. The Bible states what the relationship of husband and wife looks like.

> "Haven't you read," Jesus replied, "that at the beginning the Creator made them male and female, and said, 'For this reason a man will leave his father and mother and be united to his wife, and the two will become one flesh'? So, they are no longer two, but one flesh. Therefore, what God has joined together, let no one separate." (Matthew 19:4–6 NIV)

This is an area of the family structure that has taken a beating for decades in my experience and for centuries in the world experience. Husbands and wives who are not equally yoked in thinking about each other, children, finances, and more struggle. There are many couples where one is a person of faith and the other is not. Usually in those situations, people will be committed as long as they decide to, and they do not develop accountability. Mutual respect, like-mindedness, love, compromise, and accountability will help a marriage thrive. A husband and wife should not be afraid to be the iron that sharpens iron for each other. With mutual love and respect, it helps to shape each other into better stronger people.

In Proverbs 27:19 (NLT), it says, "As a face is reflected in water, so the heart reflects the real person." This is another verse from that same chapter of the Book of Proverbs that has made a significant impact on me and my personal character. How do we see ourselves? Are there areas in our lives that could use improvement? I would love to see myself twenty-five pounds lighter. More than that, I would love to see myself more generous and Christlike. I want God to rule in my heart, and I know that reading the Bible gives me food for my heart and soul.

According to the Evangelical Methodist Church, "Sanctifying grace draws us toward Christian perfection, which John Wesley described as a heart 'habitually filled with the love of God and for neighbor' and as 'having the mind of Christ and walking as He walked.'" The Holiness movement is a response to the power of the Holy Spirit working in the hearts of people looking for renewal and peace. It's all about holy living, which is fulfilled in our commitment to reading the Bible and living a character like Christ Jesus. One thing I must clarify is, we are not the Messiah. We cannot be him. Yet at the same time, it does not stop us from learning everything about his loving character and asking God, "O to be like thee."

Although, under the current cultural outrageousness, some people allow themselves to be whatever they want to be, no matter how hurtful to themselves and others it may eventually be. I have been the pastor of a church in Pennsylvania, and I have enjoyed it. There is a man in the church that I learn to like, and I will say his name is Neil. Neil works in a factory, and he is a quality-control manager. He comes to church almost every Sunday, and he is involved in the church events. The church has chicken barbeques and all the sides twice a year, and he is very involved in those activities. The whole community comes to buy the chicken and participate, and the church has had a good reputation in the community.

Neil is in his late forties or early fifties. Neil, like me, has parted company with his hair in his late thirties. We often laugh about the mass of hair we have had at one time in life and how that has become days gone by. Then one day, I am in the local pharmacy picking up something for me or my children when I heard, "Hi, Pastor Rick." I look around and don't recognize anyone I know.

Much to my surprise, it is a woman saying hi. I am confused, thinking, *How do I know you?* and am ready to say "Have you come to the church?" And then it hits me: it is Neil dressed as a woman with a wig and a blue dress. I can't imagine what the look on my face is like when I realize it is Neil. Neil is a cross-dresser.

Neil continues to come to church and be involved, yet everything is different between him and me from that point forward. He appreciates my confidentiality, although I know inside my heart and soul that he has secrets and was thinking God cannot see. I tactfully open opportunities for visits and conversation with Neil, but he never accepts. Part of my wonder is, How does this happen? What do people go through in life that yields them to this misinterpretation of who God has created them to be? What do ink images on the body mean?

When I have been out of relationship with God, I fantasize about singing like Elvis and being as strong as superman. That has been the world's influence over my life, which has caused me to see myself as less than what God created. The hard part is, I have an older brother that is more than willing to discredit my value to the world. Everyone has an image of corruption that the devil loves to impose upon us, and he will use whatever means he can to accomplish his purpose to destroy our image.

The devil makes a selfish decision to separate us from God, and he destroyed his beautiful image. It is his goal to do the same to everyone he can. Resist the devil and draw near to God, and you will be for what you are created to be.

Genesis 1:31 says, "God saw all that He had made, and it was very good. And there was evening, and there was morning—the sixth day." When you develop your personal relationship with God the Father, the Son, and the Holy Spirit, this will mean you too. You are created just perfectly as you are. Any number of social corruptions will challenge such a statement. Why people do what they do in various life circumstances and cultures is what anthropology is all about.

> Anthropology is the science of human beings *especially* the study of human beings and their ancestors through time and space and in relation to physical character, environmental and social relations, and culture: theology dealing with the origin, nature, and destiny of human beings.

The word *anthropology* dates back to the late 16th century, but it was not until the 19th century that it was applied to the academic discipline that now bears its name. In the United States, this field of study is typically divided into four distinct branches: physical (or biological) anthropology, archaeology, cultural (or social) anthropology, and linguistic anthropology. *Anthropology* is from the New Latin word *anthropologia* ("the study of humanity") and shares its ultimate root in Greek, *anthrōpos* ("human being"). (Merriam-Webster Incorporated, 2023)

In closing, "Who am I?" is a good question for people to ask with sincerity and humility. We should not imagine that we see through the same eyes as God. If people really want to know what to think about themselves and of each other, read the New Testament.

The Apostle Paul teaches in Romans 9: 20–21, "Who are you, a mere human being, to argue with God? Should the thing that was created say to the one who created it, 'Why have you made me like this?'" With a deeper relationship with God and a good Bible teacher, people can learn that in all circumstances of they/we are a created being, they/we are beautiful in the eyes of God.

CHAPTER 8

Under the Son

To the Jews who had believed him, Jesus said, "If you hold to my teaching, you are really my disciples. Then you will know the truth, and the truth will set you free."

"They answered him, "We are Abraham's descendants and have never been slaves of anyone. How can you say that we shall be set free?" Jesus replied, "Very truly I tell you, everyone who sins is a slave to sin. Now a slave has no permanent place in the family, but a Son belongs to it forever. So, if the Son sets you free, you will be free indeed." (John 8:31–36)

This chapter will deal with the change that occurs in the life of a believer in Christ Jesus. Like some of the Jews in this text, people of our current era like to promote their social standing in the world as if they can impress God. "They answered him, 'We are Abraham's descendants and have never been slaves of anyone. How can you say that we shall be set free?'" Have you ever produced an opinion of yourself from your social circumstances? If you are human like me, you have probably done so. What I hope to share with this audience is that God knows you from a totally different perspective, and if you welcome God's perspective, it is amazing grace for your life.

We are all slaves—slaves to the way we were brought up in this world. Have you been baptized as an infant and then talked about the great love of God everyday afterward? Have you been a child of skeptical parents or of a nonreligious society? I can ask questions about social scenarios until we are all blue in the face. My point is that I have heard of almost every social influence that has shaped the lives of people. I have heard so many stories about stern nuns applying some level of physical discipline from people who attended religious schools.

We are all slaves to the influences that cause us to have some level of doubt regarding our introduction to God the Father, the Son, and the Holy Spirit. Jesus said, "If you hold to my teaching, you are really my disciples. Then you will know the truth, and the truth will set you free." I have personally been set free from a lot of fears and prejudices that I developed due to social influences. This is why I do not criticize the doubts of the Jewish leaders in the days of Jesus; they have also been victims of their social influences. What is important to process is, that is where I was and not where I am now.

Slavery to some fears. I have been given a pocket-sized New Testament Bible at the age of eight or nine; it is the King James Version. I have not been a good reader or really interested in reading at the time. Then the Old English of that version is so clumsy to pronounce and understand, I have been frustrated. Even my parents cannot read it. All I know is, this book tells me that I am going to heaven or hell, and I have become afraid to even touch it. Fortunately, by the time I did get to reading the Bible seriously more readable versions were available.

In my teens, as my hormones are coming alive, I don't have a good basis for right and wrong decision-making. Growing up in the early sixties in a conversationally challenged home, sexuality and hormones are not discussed. Sex education classes in the school consist of pictures of the results of getting an STD. Therefore, the hormones I am created with become a fear to explore think and worry about.

After graduation, what do I do with my life? With getting married and starting a family, how much money do we need? With the statistics of divorce in the culture, will we be another statistic? And we have been. And now I have a good home and all is well, when will the bottom fall out? I share this with you hoping that you don't think I need a therapist. I share so that you will know the value of self-reflection and how God is with us through it all. When we are willing to know thyself, then we are ready for God's grace that always wins the day.

Under the Son means we are under a blanket of protection and that we will not fully understand this side of heaven. Alcohol Anonymous has a twelve-step program that members recite and reflect upon at each meeting. I was asked to lead an AA meeting at a county jail after the previous leader has left. I know nothing about leading such a meeting because I have never attended one, but it is a need the deputy warden has, to find someone to fill. He knows me because I have been visiting an inmate who is a relative of a church member where I am the pastor. I have shared the first three of the twelve steps of AA.

1. We admitted we were powerless over alcohol—that our lives had become unmanageable.
2. Came to believe that a power greater than ourselves could restore us to sanity.
3. Made a decision to turn our will and our lives over to the care of God as we understood him.

My point is this: people need to come to an understanding when the world has caused them to be out of control. I am reminding the audience of the words of the religious leaders at beginning of this chapter. "They answered Jesus, 'We are Abraham's descendants and have never been slaves of anyone. How can you say that we shall be set free?' Jesus replied, 'Very truly I tell you, everyone who sins is a slave to sin.'"

Even in this moment of denial, the religious leaders has come under the power of the Son and were resistant. In their particular situation, they have become slaves to their lifestyles. In the eyes of God, it is the same for any religious leader of any era. Does the leader think more highly of their lifestyle than they should? Are they feeding their own desires and neglecting their call to service with God and for God's people. This is the point of the text and Jesus's conversation. Remember, the grace of God will manage the errors of a faithful servant.

Now, it is not my desire to criticize the Jewish leader of that day. It is worthy to suggest that whatever walk of lifestyle we are functioning in, we will be, at times, hesitant to let God guide our footsteps and life decisions. The world and our lifestyles can enslave us by habits and personal desire, even when we think we are at the top of our game.

I have met a man who is a patient, and I am his chaplain. He is very wealthy and is a well-known television personality. He is a dementia patient with some physical challenges also. At our first meeting, he is still able to communicate well and share some exciting stories. Then in his moments of reflection, he talks about all he missed out on with his family for his career. And he adds, "I seldom went to church with them." He has become a slave to his career and personal lifestyle. I never call him a slave to the world, and yet in his somewhat demented mind, he knows he is and is feeling regret. That is what Jesus is talking about. Don't let this world own your heart and soul.

In this situation, I ask the man, "When we meet, can I bring the church to you?" And he asks how. I take my guitar, we sing some hymns, and we talk about God, his family, and his eternal life. And he is redeemed. That is how it works when you experience the grace of being under the Son. Oh, if people would just go there as soon as possible.

John 8:36 says, "Now a slave has no permanent place in the family, but a Son belongs to it forever. So, if the Son sets you free, you will be free indeed." Jesus is my vine, and I am his branch. Without Him, I can do nothing (This is taken from John 15:5). And I don't want to function without the hand and word of Jesus. Let's get this right, God the Father, (Jesus) the Son, and the Holy Spirit; this is the family referenced here. Jesus comes to invite everyone into the family of God. He is the Son; he can do this. When I have received Jesus as Savior, I am taken into the family.

Slavery is common in the days of Jesus's ministry. People can be bought and sold into slavery for a number of reasons. They may have been born as a slave, and the possibility of them remaining a slave is almost certain. People also sell their children into slavery if they feel they can support them. And people who run into hard times, either by circumstances out of their control or poor choices, choose to sell themselves into slavery.

These are some of the social circumstances that perpetuated slavery and people owning people. Jesus is describing a different type of slavery that he is very aware of: the human condition involving slavery to sin. This is at a spiritual level—the corruption, indecency, sexual immorality, and crimes against God and his people. People can become a slave to their addictions, and this type of slavery can lead to separation from God and eternal death. In Jesus's mind, this is the worse type of slavery.

In the arena of slave ownership, the slave could have opportunities for freedom. If the slave is owned by a master of faith with good character, freedom is a good possibility. God provides an opportunity and a command to release properties.

Leviticus 25: 8–13 (BSB) says, "And you shall count off seven Sabbaths of years—seven times seven years—so that the seven Sabbaths of years amount to forty-nine years." Leviticus 25:13 (BSB) says, "In this Year of Jubilee, each of you shall return to his own property."

Leviticus 25 39–41 (BSB) says, "If a countryman among you becomes destitute and sells himself to you, then you must not force him into slave labor. Let him stay with you as a hired worker or temporary resident; he is to work for you until the Year of Jubilee. Then he and his children are to be released, and he may return to his clan and to the property of his fathers." Leviticus 25:17 (NIV) says, "Do not take advantage of each other but fear your God; for I am the Lord your God."

In the Leviticus 25 texts, it is clear that God commands a time for freedom and restoration. He also intends his people to be good to one another. The point here is that God commands people to live by decency and fairness; although, it must be part of the person's personal ethic. People have argued the content of the Bible for thousands of years, and in those precarious debates and arguments, the unethical people end up doing whatever indecency and disgraceful action they choose to. People become slaves to their poor ethics, greed, and power hunger.

Even though God instills the mindset for freedom, ethical behavior, and personal transformation, there are those evil powers that can enslave the body, heart, and soul. Again, the temptation that comes into the life experience at time are like a roaring lion following people through their life endeavors.

According to *Wikipedia*, Harry Houdini, born Erich Weisz on March 24, 1874–October 31, 1926, is an American escape artist, illusionist, and stunt performer noted for his escape acts. His pseudonym is a reference to his spiritual master, French magician Robert-Houdin (1805–1871).

Harry Houdini is an interesting man for me as a young boy growing up, hearing about him and his magic and escape acts. My brothers and I try to mimic him, and we fall very short. Nonetheless, he is fascinating to us. The reason I share this with my audience is that here we have a man who is a renowned magician and escape artist, and yet his heart and soul are enslaved to limelight and to the next bigger and better act, and his life has suffered to this slavery.

John 8: 36 says, "So, if the Son sets you free, you will be free indeed." This is what Jesus wants to do for all humanity: to give us a chance to experience real freedom. Jesus is not opposed to successful people. As a matter of fact, he embraces the wealth of Matthew for his ministry.

> He went to Nazareth, where he had been brought up, and on the Sabbath day He went into the synagogue, as was his custom. He stood up to read, and the scroll of the prophet Isaiah was handed to Him. Unrolling it, He found the place where it is written: "The Spirit of the Lord is on Me, because He has anointed Me to proclaim good news to the poor. He has sent Me to pro-

> claim freedom for the prisoners and recovery of sight for the blind, to set the oppressed free, to proclaim the year of the Lord's favor." Then He rolled up the scroll, gave it back to the attendant and sat down. The eyes of everyone in the synagogue were fastened on him. He began by saying to them, "Today this scripture is fulfilled in your hearing." (Luke 4:16–21)

These are the words that Jesus has used to start his ministry. Let me remind my audience that due to the ascension, Jesus is at the right hand of the Father, where they watch carefully to continue his ministry. The Holy Spirit is sent here as our comforter, teacher, and guide until the return of Christ Jesus. With this in mind, it is appropriate to accept that Jesus's ministry is still functioning at full power.

I believe this is a text that can take a person on a power spiritual journey. First act of ministry is "to proclaim good news to the poor." Poor, in this sense, is not just financially poor; it includes poorness in the spirit. The good news is that a fresh mind and a transformed heart can set a person on a journey that causes them to accept someone to believe in. Luke 4:37 says, "For with God nothing will be impossible." "He has sent Me to proclaim freedom for the prisoners"—this is the power that triumphs over slavery of all types. "Recovery of sight for the blind" is not just to the physically blind but also to those are blind to the truth. "To set the oppressed free, to proclaim the year of the Lord's favor." God shows no favoritism, and his grace is widespread and never-ending.

> Then Mary said to the angel, "How can this be, since I do not know a man?" And the angel answered and said to her, "*The* Holy Spirit will come upon you, and the power of the Highest will overshadow you; therefore, also, that Holy One who is to be born will be called the Son of God. Now indeed, Elizabeth your relative has also conceived a son in her old age; and this is

now the sixth month for her who was called barren. For with God nothing will be impossible." Then Mary said, "Behold the maidservant of the Lord! Let it be to me according to your word." And the angel departed from her." (Luke 1:34–38 NIV; italics added)

This Scripture is a conversation between the angel Gabriel and Mary, the mother of Christ Jesus. Gabriel comes to Mary with some world-changing news. The following verses give us a clue into the glorious power that accompanies the introduction of God's Son into the world.

In the sixth month of Elizabeth's pregnancy, God sent the angel Gabriel to Nazareth, a town in Galilee, to a virgin pledged to be married to a man named Joseph, a descendant of David. The virgin's name was Mary. The angel went to her and said, "Greetings, you who are highly favored! The Lord is with you." Mary was greatly troubled at his words and wondered what kind of greeting this might be. But the angel said to her, "Do not be afraid, Mary; you have found favor with God." (Luke 1:26–30)

This is so awesome because it reveals to us the holy way in which Jesus will be introduced into everyone's life. Mary, like most people then and now, has prayed to God for restoration of their personal life and culture. And in God's perfect time, Mary's answer comes by the angel Gabriel, and the restoration is not done for her, but it was done with her. My personal conversion is awesome. God does not need to repeat the Gabriel-and-Mary scene. The most obvious reason is because Jesus is already here, and my call and purpose, though different, is in the eyes of the Lord.

> Grace and peace to you from Him who is, and who was, and who is to come, and from the seven spirits before his throne, and from Jesus Christ, who is the faithful witness, the firstborn from the dead, and the ruler of the kings of the earth. To Him who loves us and has freed us from our sins by His blood and has made us to be a kingdom and priests to serve His God and Father—to him be glory and power for ever and ever! Amen. (Revelations 1:4–6)

I share this text at this time with my audience in order to lead everyone into a new expanse with God but of deeper awareness. I have shared scriptures from the gospel moment a few thousand years ago when God sent the angel Gabriel to Mary. The Revelation text above informs us that God is the God of the past, of the present, and of the future. God can do for us and in us today very similar things, as God has done in the days past and will continue to do so in the future until Jesus returns in the last days.

I am not Mary, the mother of Jesus! Although, like her, I am called by the Holy Spirit to bring the truth of Christ Jesus in my current world. The god of the past has the same power to act in me as my god of the present. Therefore, in what seems to be an almost-impossible means in the days of Mary, God has opened up a holy experience for everyone who believes and follows. All dedicated believers can be the way that Christ Jesus plans—to be born afresh in the heart, soul, and life of someone we meet.

In the text, we learn God is omnipresent (ever present and everlasting). We also learn about the seven spirits and Christ Jesus. Seven is the number of completions in the eyes of God. The seven spirits represent a completed number of holy ones watching over God's people. The text is referring to the seven churches of the era. Although there are enough holy ones to do the job.

Continuing the Revelation 1 text, it says, "And from Jesus Christ, who is the faithful witness, the firstborn from the dead, and the ruler of the kings of the earth." Know this: God is eternal, the seven spirits I am familiar with, and Christ Jesus I follow.

We live in a five-star culture. When I research anything from Home Depot products to places to travel to or restaurants to dine at, there is a rating attached to the advertisement. The rating is usually one to five stars. If a facility gets a one- to two-star rating, we usually move on the next place. If the place receives a four- to five-star rating, we become interested. Too many people take the easy road when it comes to knowing God the Father, the Son, and the Holy Spirit. God is awesome and deserves a rating not created by the human rating system but by personal relationship and dedication.

I can give God the Father, the seven spirts, and Christ Jesus all million–star ratings. That is not the point to just take my word and leave it at that. You must find out for yourself. The rating system, the CliffsNotes, or any other shortcut to God is wrong. Now then, leave the rating systems to worldly things of less importance aside and complete your relationship with God by doing whatever it takes to experience the miraculous moments with God.

"To Him who loves us and has freed us from our sins by His blood and has made us to be a kingdom and priests to serve His God and Father—to him be glory and power for ever and ever! Amen." These closing verses of this text emphasize what it means to be under the Son. The love of Christ Jesus is not a love finished on the cross or in the resurrection. His love is eternal and in constant vigil with the seven spirits over the life of the believer. Once a person accepts Christ Jesus as their savior, there is an eternal grace over them.

Pray with me. "Lord and Christ Jesus, forgive my sins and free me for a new life direction. I want to be a child of God. In Jesus's name I pray. Amen."

If you have prayed the prayer on the previous page, you are now a child of God, and you need to find a church to support you as you move forward in your relationship with God. You are free indeed!

> So, we have stopped evaluating others from a human point of view. At one time we thought of Christ merely from a human point of view. How

> differently we know him now! This means that anyone who belongs to Christ has become a new person. The old life is gone; a new life has begun! (2 Corinthians 5:16–17)

This is a letter to the church in Corinth from the Apostle Paul. It is the second letter, and the implication is that the congregation is growing in their faith and understanding of God, which is revealed through Christ Jesus. It is important for all people new to their faith to realize we are going through a spiritual development process. I remember as a new believer, I look at people who have grown deeper in their faith. I am encouraged, while at the same time feeling, I wish I am like them. And I have had people feel that way about me. And even for the person who has been a long time in their spiritual process, we are still in the growth process too.

Under the Son means we will forever be in a spiritual growth process. John 1:40–42 says, "Andrew, Simon Peter's brother, was one of the two who heard what John had said and who had followed Jesus. The first thing Andrew did was to find his brother Simon and tell him, 'We have found the Messiah.' And he brought him to Jesus. Jesus looked at him and said, 'You are Simon son of John. You will be called Cephas' (which, when translated, is Peter)." This has been Peter's day as a new believer, and he feels very limited in his understanding of God. The following text reveals Peter's growth. Matthew 16:15–16 says, "'But what about you?' Jesus asked. 'Who do you say I am?' Simon Peter answered, 'You are the Messiah, the Son of the living God.'"

This is growth process that Jesus blesses in our lives, and we are not quite aware of how it works. And possibly, we are not aware that it is working in our lives at all. As a matter of fact, for many people, the process is so subtle that until something miraculous happens in their lives, they don't sense it. Think about your own growth processes for a moment.

I have joined a square dance group many years ago because it looks like fun. The first class is a mishmash of switching directions, switching partners, and all of it is happening too fast for me to keep up. I feel like everyone is looking at me, and I am like the ball in a dodge ballgame, being thrown here and there. Eventually I learn the dance moves and the caller's instruction and look at all the newbies and grinned.

In a similar way, we need to stay in the dance (relationship) with Jesus, and we will learn why we are doing what we are doing. We will get to the place where we understand his voice calling out to us. Think of it this way: in Genesis 2: 15–17, it says, "The Lord God took the man and put him in the Garden of Eden to work it and take care of it. And the Lord God commanded the man, 'You are free to eat from any tree in the garden; but you must not eat from the tree of the knowledge of good and evil, for when you eat from it you will certainly die.'"

God is not trying to keep Adam ignorant. Instead, he wants Adam to trust that he will reveal to him in the appropriate time all the information he needs to know about good and evil. And we learn that Adam doesn't keep the command. This is why Jesus reveals to us the growth process when we are ready to understand it. Jesus is not willing to let chaos happen to us again when we are going through the spiritual growth process. Someone might dare call Jesus a control freak—shame on them if they do. Jesus knows and feels the cost for setting humanity free on the cross, and that is a price he does not want anyone else to feel.

The Apostle Paul knows firsthand the spiritual growth process ordained upon his life through Christ Jesus. Acts 9 tells the story of Saul meeting Jesus on the road to Damascus after Jesus has been resurrected. Saul's life is so extremely different in this spiritual growth process that he changes his name to Paul. In the following text, Paul shares with his readers just how important this whole new life in Christ Jesus really is.

> And all of this is a gift from God, who brought us back to himself through Christ. And God has given us this task of reconciling people to him. For God was in Christ, reconciling the world to himself, no longer counting people's sins against

them. And he gave us this wonderful message of reconciliation. So, we are Christ's ambassadors; God is making his appeal through us. We speak for Christ when we plead, "Come back to God!" For God made Christ, who never sinned, to be the offering for our sin, so that we could be made right with God through Christ. (2 Corinthians 5:18–21)

Paul is a Pharisee in the Jewish culture; he is the best of the best. Paul knows the Jewish standards and rituals, and he knows the Law of Moses and the words of the Psalms and of the prophets. Paul also knows that the animal sacrifices made in the temple have become a mockery of the commands of God and that no one is set right with God through these meaningless, horrific displays. The sacrifices are meant to reconcile a person/family/culture to God.

Some people are very spiritual and become dedicated to the rituals and sacred gifts of God, such as baptism and Holy Communion. The sacraments mean so much to me, and I praise God for the right to experience them. And yet I have attended church services that set the communion elements to the side, and if you want to take you can and if not, no problem. These churches are mocking the ritual of God that is intended to remind us that Christ Jesus has died for us.

And the previous words are the evidence of the spiritual growth process in a person/church/culture or the lack of it. "We speak for Christ when we plead, 'Come back to God!'" What Paul is getting at here is the rituals of the past that has made a mockery of God's commands and has not lead people back to God. Jesus will use us to say "Come back to God" until the time he returns. And Paul teaches just what we are to teach. "For God made Christ, who never sinned, to be the offering for our sin, so that we could be made right with God through Christ."

We must participate in the sacraments as dedicated and spiritually growing people. If we do not, it is no different than what happened to the animal sacrifices. They have ended, but God no longer accepts them. We are only made right with God through Christ

Jesus. Therefore, every participation in the sacraments needs to be an act that reveals the participant's spiritual growth process. If a person participates in the sacraments with unholy thoughts and actions, they are making a mockery of Jesus, and they are in risk of a curse. That does not give us the right to curse someone; it only requires us to inform people when they are walking away from grace.

While I am serving as pastor of a church, a woman calls and wants to set a meeting with me to discuss the baptism of her child. I willing agree and set the appointment. The woman arrives with her child who was sleeping. She says, "I am a witch, and I practice wiccan rituals."

I am shocked and then ask, "Do you believe in God the Father, the Son, and the Holy Spirit?"

She replies, "I'm not into religious stuff."

I then ask, "Why do you want your child to be baptized?"

She replies, "So that he will be a warlock with God."

I say, "I won't do that, and I would warn you of a curse you may be subjecting your child to."

She said, "Okay, I will find someone else."

This is how holy rituals and sacred moments with God are treated at times.

On the previous page, I shared with the readers that it is a command/expectation of God that people respect the sacred gifts of God. This is not an invented language of priests and pastors; it is the will of God. Priests, pastors, all clergy, lay leaders, Christians, and all religious people fall under this call to respect the rituals of God. I am going to use a text from an Old Testament prophet Ezekiel to remind us of the will and character of God.

> Then another message came to me from the Lord: "Why do you quote this proverb concerning the land of Israel: 'The parents have eaten sour grapes, but their children's mouths pucker at the taste'? As surely as I live, says the Sovereign Lord, you will not quote this proverb anymore in Israel. For all people are mine to judge—both

> parents and children alike. And this is my rule: The person who sins is the one who will die." (Ezekiel 18:1–4 NLT)

Remember, the character of God has been revealed and fulfilled through the life and ministry of Christ Jesus too. Let's get the idea of this text. People are saying the bad that we are doing, we are getting away with. But too bad that our kids will have to answer for it. And what was even worse is the idea that the next generation is a little farther away from the promises of God—who cares. I think our culture has fallen into that insane trap of the devil. What happens with people of loose ethics is that they are distant from God, and they want everyone to go to hell with them.

And that is not how it works with the will of God. This is a disgrace in the presence of God. People cannot act without their actions being recorded in the book of life in the kingdom of God. Those who have worked in good behavior will live forever. Those who have worked in bad behavior will die. This is all a matter of the heart, soul, and spirit. I have many men thank me for my jail ministry, and they live. I have some men spit at me, and they either have repented or died in their sins.

The people that rejects me are not the problem. They reject the one who sent me, Christ Jesus. The Scriptures are revealing to us that God has his eye on all people and all generations.

Under the Son means to us that God of the Old Testament reveals and fulfills his purpose to the world through the Messiah and Christ Jesus. Jesus judges people on their own actions and nothing else. Therefore, if anyone thinks my parents are Jews, Catholic, Lutheran, Presbyterian, Methodist, Baptist, United Church of Christ, Nazarene, or whatever the title may have in mind and that we are okay, think again. These Scriptures reveal to everyone that we are all accountable to God. Sincere humility is necessary for a healthy relationship with God.

> "What?" you ask. "Doesn't the child pay for the parent's sins?" No! For if the child does what is

> just and right and keeps My decrees, that child will surely live. The person who sins is the one who will die. The child will not be punished for the parent's sins, and the parent will not be punished for the child's sins. Righteous people will be rewarded for their own righteous behavior, and wicked people will be punished for their own wickedness. But if wicked people turn away from all their sins and begin to obey my decrees and do what is just and right, they will surely live and not die. All their past sins will be forgotten, and they will live because of the righteous things they have done. (Ezekiel 18:19–22)

Here is a quandary for the soul. How do we do what is right? Are we confident that we have lived a good life and that we are right with God? Everyone that is subject to the calamity called life are led into unrighteousness. It is not our impression of our conduct and actions that lead us to heaven; it is God's impression of our conduct and actions. The only way to learn about God's impression of the human character is to study the character of Christ Jesus. We can't blame anyone else for our lack of Christlike character.

> Therefore, I will judge each of you, O people of Israel, according to your actions, says the Sovereign Lord. Repent, and turn from your sins. Don't let them destroy you! Put all your rebellion behind you and find yourselves a new heart and a new spirit. For why should you die, O people of Israel? I don't want you to die, says the Sovereign Lord. Turn back and live! (Ezekiel 18:30–32 NLT)

Can you hear the compassion of God in these words? Can you hear the Lord speaking directly to you, and have you heard words like this or felt the enticing Spirit of God calling you into whole new life? I am appalled with people suggesting that God is not gracious, loving, and forgiving. God is ready to lead everyone in a path of righteousness.

There is another part of this scripture that may seem pushy or too religious. And that is "Repent, and turn from your sins. Don't let them destroy you! Put all your rebellion behind you and find yourselves a new heart and a new spirit." The keyword here is *repent*. *Repent* means to turn from the current direction you are going in and to go the other way. The fascinating part about this concept is that we usually do it many times in our life. People change directions in relationships, jobs, hair color, and education. So what we are actually hearing from God is common sense advice. You all know when you have been on a dead-end course and finally decide to go a different direction, get out of the situation, and so on. God wants us on the best path.

"Turn back and live!" The above verses end with these words. Some people know the story of God and his children being separated in the Garden of Eden. Sin has separated them. It is not Adam's or Eve's race or religion that caused the separation; it is the presence of sin. God loves us. We are his children. It is sin that is a problem.

> When you were slaves to sin, you were free from the obligation to do right. And what was the result? You are now ashamed of the things you used to do, things that end in eternal doom. But now you are free from the power of sin and have become slaves of God. Now you do those things that lead to holiness and result in eternal life. For the wages of sin is death, but the free gift of God is eternal life through Christ Jesus our Lord. (Romans 6:20–23 NIV)

The above scripture is a chapter in a letter from the Apostle Paul to the church in Rome. He is trying to help the people to come to terms with their new lifestyles and character and to also understand the corrupt societies we are born into are the results of sin. In Paul's teachings, he knows some people are slaves and some are not but that all people are slaves to the sin plaguing our societies.

Whether we are willing to consider the world chaos, people harming one another, and all the destructive events perpetuated in our society or not, they are occurring every day. Every prophet from Moses to Jesus and the disciples and apostles are teaching sin and chaos are not the will of God. Think about common sense—"Do unto others as you would have them do to you." You may think about this only from a biblical stance or not. Yet 95 percent of the people I have met as a pastor or chaplain believe this the correct way to live. If you don't like the word *sin*, then use immorality. Either way, they need to be removed from the person and the society.

Many years ago, I have been employed part-time at a Dollar General store. When I have been going through the orientation process, the biggest losses for the store is stolen goods. And a large percentage of those stolen goods are stolen by the employees. That is just one fact of how sin and immorality are hurting our society. God is not planning religious groups; he is planning personal relationship with righteousness as a tool of inspiration and encouragement.

Sin and immorality are hurting our human society. There are cultures including our own where stealing from one another is common place and a way of getting more. I challenge all the evolutionists and their theories that we are not created but evolved into what we currently are. Society has been on a destructive, degenerating movement that would have abolished everything if it were not for the influence of God the creator, Jesus the Son, and the Holy Spirit. It is important that we accept we are part of the problem due to the influence of sin in our culture.

It is also important to acknowledge the great advances that have occurred in our society and that continue to do so. In the area of technology and medicine, we have witnessed amazing accomplishments. In technology, we have the media, the computer, and the cell phones—not forgetting to mention all the programs and apps that assist these devices. As a chaplain for a medical team, the computer has made medical charting easier and faster.

In the field of medicine, surgeries and medications have saved and extended lives for millions of people. I remember the discussion and news about open heart-surgery and the first successful heart transplant in December 1967. In my years of chaplain ministries, about 80 percent of doctors and nurses are faith-based people, feeling they are doing the work of God for people.

Therefore, I prefer the word *developed* instead of *evolved*. The great accomplishment in our society is a partnership of blessings between God and his people. This is not accidental. It is a purposeful transformation of our society. When humanity is left to the theory of functioning as instinctual animals, it's truly an insult to who we are created in the image of God. Jesus reveals to the world the power of God at work in the hands of his Son. He heals, casts out spiritual demons, and raises people to life. And if that are not enough, Jesus has passed this power on to seventy-two disciples and sent them out to help others.

> So I find this law at work: Although I want to do good, evil is right there with me. For in my inner being I delight in God's law; but I see another law at work in me, waging war against the law of my mind and making me a prisoner of the law of sin at work within me. What a wretched man I am! Who will rescue me from this body that is subject to death? Thanks be to God, who delivers me through Jesus Christ our Lord! (Romans 7:21–25 NIV)

The above text is a good example of self-reflection. I have mentioned this idea in previous chapters, and it is important to remember self-reflection is an ongoing endeavor. It doesn't have to be a "woe is me" conversation in the soul. I have often arrived at the place in my soul when I have said "Thank you, God, I got through that stuff." We need to read the words above from the Apostle Paul as a moment of relief—"I have been delivered out of this mess by faith in the power of Christ Jesus."

Have you ever said to yourself or someone else "I'm a good person. I have not intentionally done anything that bad"? I have said that, so don't make me feel alone here. If you really have said or thought that for real, I suggest you unzip the bubble you are living in and come out into the real world. Like what Paul said in the text above, I want to do right and be a good person, but then this good person gets pulled into a world environment that does not bring out the best in him. I have learned to have peace and actually rejoice in the realm that God has used me to do something really good. I would rather be an instrument in the hand of God and think he has considered me worthy to use than to pat myself on the back.

If you wonder about putting this into perspective, consider this. I have been a runner in school, and in one track meet, our team placed first, second, and third, and we won. I was the third-place runner. Everyone thought it was great a sweep. Then one person asked, "Why weren't you first?"

Which voice do you think has been the loudest in my heart and soul: all the praises of the well-meaning people or the one negative voice? The negative voice wins out. That is the predicament we can get into when we want to have the "good person" title. Something in this weird world will throw a monkey wrench into our happy place.

> The apostle Paul wrote, "I have been crucified with Christ and I no longer live, but Christ lives in me. This verse speaks to the idea that when we accept Jesus Christ as our Savior, we are no longer living by ourselves but with Him. We are called to live by faith and to allow Christ to work through us. This is a powerful reminder that we are not alone in this world and that we have a purpose beyond ourselves." (Galatians 2:20)

I share this with you with the intention of moving us into the last part of this chapter. We can resist faithful people that God sends our way and take the low road thinking, *I don't need God or anyone else. I am the master of my destination.* But without God in your life, you will be the master of your eternal destruction. I am not saying this as a religious person who desires to condemn anyone. I don't have the power or right to judge or condemn. I say this as a person who is loved by God and his people and has become part of the family of God. I want you there too.

Jesus is God in the flesh, and he has come here to walk, work, serve, and save. I have much to share with you about the spiritual opportunities opened to me/us as people walking this life journey with Jesus. I also know from personal experience that all the great riches of heaven are available for us when we accept Jesus as the way to God and heaven. To the person who lives only to gratify their personal desires, God and heaven may be the farthest thing from their minds. I have been with many people who want a crash course on faith and eternal life. And often, it is not a pleasant journey of moving from self-centeredness to truth with God.

Not all is lost in this endeavor. One of the skills/gifts God has equipped me with is the compassion to walk the end-life journey with people and help them separate world from heaven. I would be the first to tell you I feel ill-equipped for this service. As a matter of fact, I resist the service when I can. I do not resist because I don't see the validity in the service, but I tend to resist because I wonder if it will it work and if I will be effective. This is what the Apostle Paul is talking about. I am not always on board with what I know I should do; therefore, I see a battle at work in me. You will experience this too. Have you ever said to yourself, "I hate going to the dentist," and yet you decide to go anyway? Join my club.

> Then Jesus went with his disciples to a place called Gethsemane, and He said to them, "Sit here while I go over there and pray." He took Peter and the two sons of Zebedee along with him, and he began to be sorrowful and troubled. Then He said to them, "My soul is overwhelmed with sorrow to the point of death. Stay here and keep watch with me." Going a little farther, He fell with his face to the ground and prayed, "My

> Father, if it is possible, may this cup be taken from Me. Yet not as I will, but as You will." (Matthew 26:36–39 NIV)

Here it is, brothers and sisters, the Messiah who came to save the world had his own struggles as he dealt with chaos of the world. In his own moments of human heartbreak, he has not been not willing to surrender to his personal desire. We are not called to be the Messiah. Jesus has had a moment of humanness, just like us, but also had his moment of overcoming the world. We should see this as a Holy Spirit moment, that when in the hard times, the Spirit comes along side of us to comfort and sustain us in the moment of struggle. This is the beauty of giving your life over to Jesus. Now pray and ask him into your heart and to forgive your sins, and the process of new life begins.

> For this reason I kneel before the Father, from whom every family in heaven and on earth derives its name. I pray that out of his glorious riches he may strengthen you with power through his Spirit in your inner being, so that Christ may dwell in your hearts through faith. And I pray that you, being rooted and established in love, may have power, together with all the Lord's holy people, to grasp how wide and long and high and deep is the love of Christ, and to know this love that surpasses knowledge—that you may be filled to the measure of all the fullness of God. (Ephesians 3:14–19 NIV)

The above scripture are the words of the Apostle Paul in a letter to the church in Ephesus. This is the benefit of receiving the Lord and Christ Jesus as your savior. That is why I invite those who have not prayed and asked Jesus to come into their life on the previous page. The Apostle Paul's words are so precise regarding the amazing difference a life with Jesus makes. This is the example of God's love and grace that we cannot get in any other relationship known to humanity. We are now under the Son and with all the riches of heaven. I am eager to share with my audiences my rich experiences of the heavenly glories and my deep love for God the Father, the Son, and the Holy Spirit. That will be a different writing, if God so desires.

> Now to him who is able to do immeasurably more than all we ask or imagine, according to His power that is at work within us, to Him be glory in the church and in Christ Jesus throughout all generations, for ever and ever! Amen. (Ephesians 3:20–21 NIV)

I close this chapter with this prayer of the Apostle Paul, and I ask you to read them over and over again so that they are sealed by God in your heart, soul, and mind. And may the peace that passes all understanding guard your heart and soul in Christ Jesus now and forever. Amen.

CHAPTER 9

The Weight Is Lifted

I lift up my eyes to the mountains, where does my help come from?

My help comes from the Lord, the Maker of heaven and earth. He will not let your foot slip.

He who watches over you will not slumber; indeed, He who watches over Israel will neither slumber nor sleep.

The Lord watches over you; the Lord is your shade at your right hand; the sun will not harm you by day, nor the moon by night. The Lord will keep you from all harm.

He will watch over your life; the Lord will watch over your coming and going both now and forevermore. (Psalm 121:1–8)

These words are put to music as a music to worship the Lord. These are used in the Jewish temple and synagogues. For the current-day Christian, much of the Old Testament is very inspirational. The Book of Psalms is almost like a prayer book. I have put my own music to these words with my guitar. The words are meant to comfort your soul and lift your spirit into a place of everlasting support from God.

I wanted to use the scripture to start this chapter "The Weight Is Lifted." I have been a pastor for over twenty-five years and a believer/

Christian even longer. Therefore, my purpose is to enlighten your heart and soul to the immense grace of God. With that said, I also have spent a lot of time with my feet on the ground, and that perpetuates good moments and bad ones too. In other words, I know what it's like to suffer and struggle. I also know what it's like to overcome the struggle with God and God's people. I am hoping you have prayed the prayer from previous chapters to receive Jesus as your Lord and Savior. Let me share my personal place in this arena. As a child, I have heard about the judgement and the commands of God. I have never heard the word *grace*. I suspect judgment and commands have been to keep me behaving.

Now I don't want you to get the wrong idea, like I have been a misbehaving child. It has been my twin brother's fault. My point here is that no one escapes the challenge of a corrupt society and the complications it can produce. For so many years, I have believed I am doomed to hell because I can't stop sinning. As a born-again believer, I have learned that I am not doomed but saved by faith in God's grace revealed in Christ Jesus, and I am relieved.

This is what the prayer is about from the previous chapter. It is all about when we ask Jesus to be Lord of our life and forgive our sins and the sins are removed. I can't do it; only Jesus can. I'm going to try to put this in terms that don't sound super religious. Reading the New Testament—Matthew, Mark, Luke, and John—I learned about the character and power of Jesus. I have learned he is pure and without sin because he is the Son of God, and his Spirit does not sin. In Matthew 4, we can read how the devil tries to tempt Jesus to sin, but it does not happen. And the devil leaves with his tail between his legs.

Get this, Jesus is sinless and pure, and he came to earth to lift the weight of sin. Only a sinless savior can complete such a task. Let me give you a limited comparison. Two boys grow up together and are very close friends. One boy goes on to become a lawyer, and the other, a thief. On one legal occasion years later, they are reunited. One is now a judge, the other, the criminal. They both recognize each other. The criminal feels ashamed in front of his friend from the past. The judge has the responsibility to hear the terms and maintain the law in the matter. He sentences the criminal with a fine suitable to the crime. The judge then takes off his robe, goes into his chambers, and writes a check to pay his longtime friend's fine. That is what Jesus does in a most outstanding way. He lifts the weight of sin off from the shoulders of all people who accepts him and believes in his power.

Now think about this. The man who has his fine paid is set free to live and let the gift of another change his life. We are in that same boat. Jesus has paid the price for us, and now we are given the gift to live a life not weighted down by sin. Now for the person who is looking for a better direction in life, the idea of not being condemned is wonderful. And for the person who is not sure which life they want to lead, they may pass over their new life direction.

The difference between these two people is, one is looking for relief from the traps and chaos of the world that weigh them down and the other is in denial. As a pastor and chaplain, I have visited with people who are homeless AIDS victims, people who are honored military leaders, and everything in between. They all need the weight lifted off their body, heart, and soul.

Everyone is challenged with the temptation of "I am my own person." Most people learn their limitations and seek help from God and faithful professional Christian counselors. Now I am not claiming that those who confessed their limitations are people who are ready to stand on the street corner and do so. In 90 percent of the cases, it is quiet personal reflection with me because they trusted me. Nevertheless, the weight is lifted. My personal desire for all people is that they let Jesus lift the weight off from them sooner rather than later.

This is an area where I know there is a constant need for love and grace—that is the stubborn person who believes there is always more time. This is the person who uses denial as a coping mechanism. As a chaplain, I comforted families during hospice situations. The patient usually reaches the place of acceptance of limited world experience and looks for guidance to the heaven experience. I would pray, teach, quote scripture, and provide Christlike comfort. The family members watch with amazement the peace that occurs. And many of the families looking on in amazement have never accepted someday that might be me.

The point here is the sooner the weight is lifted the better. My weight has been lifted over thirty years ago, and it has caused me to live a life more focused on grace than chaos, a point of conversation and clarification. I want to define what "the weight is lifted" means in my heart, mind, and soul. For the longtime believer or the new believer, there is something to be gained in these words.

Martin Luther, the founder of the Lutheran Church, is a fascinating man. He is a Catholic monk/priest for years and has had a spiritual struggle in his life. He goes to confession, confesses his sin, and then on the way back to his room, he sins again and run back to the confessional. The priest hearing his confessions gets a little tired of his obsession with being sinless. In his frustration, he returns to his room to read the Bible and prays, and he opens the Bible to Romans 1:17 (NIV), which says, "The righteous will live by faith." He realizes faith in God is the answer, and the worry and weight are lifted.

This is for the less religious. I have been serving as a chaplain in a county jail in Pennsylvania. I meet a man who I will call Mike. He is from a prominent family, and he has an addiction to meth. He is also known to cook it and sell it. He is a target for the local and state police. When the police catches and arrests him, they are hoping to learn about his distribution and bigger players. Because he is at home with his wife and children, they arrest her and him and take the children to her parents. The wife is an innocent bystander. The police thinks that he will give up his system and contacts for his wife's release.

He holds out for a while, and then I get a request from his wife to visit her. She says, "Tell him if he does not confess and tell them what is needed to get me out, my family will kill him." I tell him, and he believes. He confesses, and the weight is lifted.

Then he is placed in a confinement cell where no one can get to him, and he has a twenty-four-hour watch. When he confesses and shares his information, his wife is set free, and he feels right. As time goes by and I visit Mike, he tell me of the day he has prayed for Jesus to save him. Mike and his wife eventually separate and divorce. He is sentenced to several years, and he wants his wife to move on with the children. The weight of addiction and the chaos that goes with it are lifted off from Mike, and he reclaims his relationship with Christ Jesus.

What is the weight you are carrying? Not everyone has the troubling life circumstances like Mike. Nevertheless, whatever our circumstances are, do they perpetuate worry and concern? And do they weigh you down? For example, as a pastor, there is always the concern of the church leaders of "how do we pay our bills and do more." My work is to get the church to not keep up with the Joneses, not to compare their church ministry and influence to other churches. And then there are the braggers—"Our church did this or that, and we were amazing." It always reminds me of kids in school bragging about their dads or their pets, whichever they like more.

The successes of any ministry are to be credited to the power of God helping his people and churches. And yet they carry this unnecessary, imaginary weight. Do you have friends that seem to always one-up you? Do you have thoughts that you are cursed and not equal with others? Forget those ideas, for God shows no favoritism. Deuteronomy 10:17 says, "For the Lord your God is God of gods and Lord of lords, the great God, mighty and awesome, who shows no partiality and accepts no bribes." When you get in your mind that God does not compare you to anyone else, you can gradually stop comparing yourself to others. There are many amazing preachers and teachers in this world, but they do not have the same message to share as I do. The weight of comparison needs to be lifted off your shoulders. We are all an individual creation of God.

> So, Pharaoh sent for Joseph, and he was quickly brought from the dungeon. When he had shaved and changed his clothes, he came before Pharaoh. Pharaoh said to Joseph, "I had a dream, and no one can interpret it. But I have heard it said of you that when you hear a dream you can interpret it." "I cannot do it," Joseph replied to

Pharaoh, "but God will give Pharaoh the answer he desires." (Genesis 41:14–16)

I share this Old Testament scripture with the audience to remind everyone we are children of the God who was, who is, and who is to come. If you are to make yourself familiar with this story of Joseph, you will quickly learn an example of a good person being mistreated. Joseph is favored by his father, Jacob, because of his loyal heart and character. Joseph, being one of the younger of the twelve sons of Jacob, is hated by his brothers for his good character. His brothers sell him into slavery and tell their father, Jacob, he has been killed by a lion.

Their jealousy leads them into to sin and corruption against their own brother. I have had people ask me, Why does God let bad things happen to good people? In this situation and millions of others like them, the only way God could have stopped the bad from happening is to take away the free will of Joseph, his brothers, and everyone else in humanity. What God encourages us to do is to have faith in him and that he will redeem the situation one way or another.

In Joseph's case, he is in prison because he is wrongly accused by the pharaoh's wife. And at just the right time, God redeems the life experience of Joseph and then reveals to the pharaoh just how valuable Joseph is. In the rest of the story, Joseph is used by God and tells pharaoh what the dream means, and then Joseph goes from prison to second-in-command. Because Joseph is faithful to God, everything he does turns out good. The weight that is lifted off from Joseph is the "why me" syndrome. He learns God loves him even when those close to him don't.

Are you feeling like you get more problems than other people? If that is the case, my thoughts and prayers are with you. I want you to learn from the previous story of Joseph that God is not against you. Social jealousies and nonfaithful people are in your midst. I once have had a leader in the church say to me, "I will lie in any way I need to, to keep my power and position." Can you imagine saying that to your pastor? And that person have done just that. The only problem is that their life is doomed for eternal damnation. Remember, friends, we have horrible people in the world who will make our lives miserable. And they are not sanctioned by God, but they are actually the enemy of God. It's not you!

The weight you need lifted off from you is the weight of uncertainty. Uncertainty, aka doubt, creeps into the heart, mind, and soul and perpetuates problems. In the heart, you can feel you are not loved and are alone. I have experienced the heart of God touching my heart. It's amazing and life refreshing. When you feel okay with God, the world kind of seems less challenging while, at the same time, more lovable. And then real love has come to me because I have been lovable and not full of doubt.

Is doubt or fear something to be judgmental about? No! Remember, we are not called to judge. Although, there is again a subject for us to consider: discernment. What this really boils down to is gracious common sense. God is gracious and calls us to be gracious to others. Discernment is common sense. It requires not making quick decisions that we might regret and requires us to think on this. When you have a faithful spouse or friend you can talk with, they may very well help you to find the best decision.

I have counted on prayer and the insights of my spouse and many church leaders to help me make the best decision. Yet you will never lose the wet blanket of doubt on earth.

> Now Thomas (also known as Didymus), one of the Twelve, was not with the disciples when Jesus came. So, the other disciples told him, "We have seen the Lord!" But he said to them, "Unless I see the nail marks in his hands and put my finger where the nails were, and put my hand into his side, I will not believe." A week later his disciples were in the house again, and Thomas was with them. Though the doors were locked, Jesus came and stood among them and said, "Peace be with you!" Then he said to Thomas, "Put your finger here; see my hands. Reach out your hand and

put it into my side. Stop doubting and believe." Thomas said to him, "My Lord and my God!" Then Jesus told him, "Because you have seen me, you have believed; blessed are those who have not seen and yet have believed." I repeat this doubt story for our moment in grace. (John 20:24–29)

The company of the prophets said to Elisha, "Look, the place where we meet with you is too small for us. Let us go to the Jordan, where each of us can get a pole; and let us build a place there for us to meet." And he said, "Go." Then one of them said, "Won't you please come with your servants?" "I will," Elisha replied. And he went with them. They went to the Jordan and began to cut down trees. As one of them was cutting down a tree, the iron ax head fell into the water. "Oh no, my lord!" he cried out. "It was borrowed!" The man of God asked, "Where did it fall?" When he showed him the place, Elisha cut a stick and threw it there, and made the iron float. "Lift it out," he said. Then the man reached out his hand and took it. (2 Kings 6:1–7 NIV)

The two scriptures above are examples of circumstances people have been in at one time or another. First, we have a tendency to doubt the truth of God because the world is full of chaos. Second, we all need to have our problems lifted. Let me explain this.

Thomas struggles with doubt because he is hurting over the loss of his teacher, master, and savior. He has never experienced a relationship with God in such a personal way, and due to the crucifixion, it has been gone in his mind. In this moment, his heartbreak needs a moment with God. And Jesus provides just that. Even though Thomas has doubts, he also returns to his friends the other disciples, and by doing so, it is love in the eyes of Jesus. We all can make a sincere act of love for our savior who died for us, and who knows, maybe a visit from your savior will renew your hope in eternity.

In the second text, the axe floats. This is the ultimate witness of God lifting the weight of problems off our lives. The amazing gift of God the Father, the Son, and the Holy Spirit is to be all present and all knowing. In this text, we have a man upset over losing a borrowed axe. He is trusted with a tool that is critical to the craftsmen of the era. And the man approaches Elisha, the man of God, for help. Remember, Elisha has a double portion of the Holy Spirit of God for conducting his ministry. And what he wants is to be an effective servant of God. The miracle occurs, and the axe head is retrieved from the river.

Now you have the option of leaving this story in the Old Testament and an event of the past. On the other hand, you have this opportunity to open your mind to a deeper meaning of the work of God. For the man who retrieves the axe head, it is a relief to be able to continue to stand as a trustworthy person. God knows about every challenge that may leave us at the mercy of other people. The point of this text is, What kind of person do you want to be? Is respectability important to you, or have you accepted the character of a crooked used-car salesman. The man of the text desires to be right and decent, and his only hope for accomplishing that is with God. The devil at every moment is looking to change the image of God given us all.

I want to close this chapter with a scripture and a valuable piece of insight I have accepted over the years. I want to share that I have heard about many philosophies of social equalization. What I mean is thoughts like karma, "what goes around comes around." That idea is, if you do bad, bad will come back and get you sooner or later. And on the other side of the coin, if you do good, good will come back to you sooner or later. Well, that leaves a lot of room for chaos. My insight is, that kind of thinking does not work out.

Everything is a personal choice. If you want to be a person of character like Christ Jesus, you must choose to do so. I have done that, and I can tell you it has worked out with faithful people. With evil people, there is always a struggle. Remember, you have the protection of God. Seek God and Christlike character, and blessing will come to you. God lifts the weight and makes life new.

> Jesus entered Jericho and was passing through. A man was there by the name of Zacchaeus; he was a chief tax collector and was wealthy. He wanted to see who Jesus was, but because he was short, he could not see over the crowd. So, he ran ahead and climbed a sycamore-fig tree to see him, since Jesus was coming that way. When Jesus reached the spot, he looked up and said to him, "Zacchaeus, come down immediately. I must stay at your house today." So, he came down at once and welcomed him gladly. All the people saw this and began to mutter, "He has gone to be the guest of a sinner." But Zacchaeus stood up and said to the Lord, "Look, Lord! Here and now, I give half of my possessions to the poor, and if I have cheated anybody out of anything, I will pay back four times the amount." Jesus said to him, "Today salvation has come to this house, because this man, too, is a son of Abraham. For the Son of Man came to seek and to save the lost." (Luke 19:1–10 (NIV)

Are you afraid to put your life in the hands of God? Get over it and enjoy life.

CHAPTER 10

Multiple Grace

And the Word became flesh and dwelt among us, and we have seen His glory, glory as of the only Son from the Father, full of grace and truth. (John bore witness about him, and cried out, "This was He of whom I said, 'He who comes after me ranks before me, because He was before me.'") For from His fullness, we have all received, grace upon grace. For the law was given through Moses; grace and truth came through Jesus Christ. No one has ever seen God; the only God who is at the Father's side, He has made him known. (John 1:14–18 ESV)

I want to share my insight and experience with grace. Grace is not earned; it is an unmerited favor from God. Now it is possible that a person inclined to personal recognition can misinterpret grace. There are many levels of God's grace. First is prevenient grace, or the grace of God working in your life before you are aware of it.

God usually leads a person to us that will help us understand the presence of God in the early stages. For me, it is a pastor with the heart for loving God's people. During my years of jail ministry, the inmates are flabbergasted that a pastor comes to help them through their challenging tines. The point here is to imagine that it is coincidence and not an act of God. God's grace is much more wonderful and loving than we can perceive. We are not the holy ones, so we need to get over the confusion.

My experience is that I have known God has called me, but I have had so few people to help me. My step-grandfather has been a man of faith but has not been equipped to lead me. His character is an inspiration, and that is all I have. Consequently, my development toward God wanes. At the age of nineteen, a friend has needed a place to stay, and I can accommodate him. He is a born-again Christian. We talk about God and pray, and that is prevenient grace preventing me from leaving the fold of God and providing me moments of strength and love.

Second is justifying grace. That is the work of God done for us as Christ Jesus suffering on the cross. Through all the legal and temple sacrifices, God knows that people are going through the motions and not really inclined to the point of knowing why they are doing what they are doing. What God proves to us is that in this chaotic world, we struggle to be committed. Then at the right time, Jesus dies for all humanity to atone for our sins and put us right with God when we believe.

When we are capable of accepting that we can't win our place with God on our own merits, then we appreciate what the sacrifice of Christ Jesus have done for us. It is at this point that sanctifying grace begins its work in us. I am totally convinced that I cannot work my way into heaven and eternal life. It would have been presumptuous of me to think I know as much as God. I cannot sanctify myself. That is like trying to give yourself an achievement award. Everyone knows that you set the standards, and that is too lame. Look to God for guidance.

And we move from sanctifying grace to perfecting grace. Perfecting grace does not come to its fulfillment on the earthly journey. We are perfected when we see the Trinity face-to-face in heaven. The awesome part of perfecting grace is that it is another work of God's grace in our lives when we believe God is in our lives through the Holy Spirit. Perfecting grace is holy and mysterious. That means we are not in control, and we cannot manipulate the grace of God.

It is a free gift for those who believe in the righteous work of Christ Jesus for the sins of all people.

In this world, we feel we are in control of our own destinations, and for a limited time, God will let us think that. And when push comes to shove and we want eternity, that means God takes over. As a hospice chaplain, I have watched people in that position many times. Serving in that arena requires grace and compassion for others, and that is bestowed by God grace also.

> Jesus entered Jericho and was passing through. A man was there by the name of Zacchaeus; he was a chief tax collector and was wealthy. He wanted to see who Jesus was, but because he was short, he could not see over the crowd. So, he ran ahead and climbed a sycamore-fig tree to see him, since Jesus was coming that way. When Jesus reached the spot, he looked up and said to him, "Zacchaeus, come down immediately. "I must stay at your house today." So, he came down at once and welcomed him gladly. All the people saw this and began to mutter, "He has gone to be the guest of a sinner." But Zacchaeus stood up and said to the Lord, "Look, Lord! Here and now, I give half of my possessions to the poor, and if I have cheated anybody out of anything, I will pay back four times the amount." Jesus said to him, "Today salvation has come to this house, because this man, too, is a son of Abraham. For the Son of Man came to seek and to save the lost." (Luke 19:1–10)

I repeat this scripture because it is a good example of the components of God's grace. Prevenient grace is what created the hunger in Zacchaeus's heart to want to see Jesus. It also inspires the idea to climb the tree. Justifying grace is when Jesus stops and says, "I must stay at your house today." It's the grace that causes people to respond.

It is an outward act from inward change—"So, he came down at once and welcomed him gladly."

Sanctifying grace is the grace of God that causes the new life and repenting character. "Look, Lord! Here and now, I give half of my possessions to the poor, and if I have cheated anybody out of anything, I will pay back four times the amount."

Perfecting grace is the grace of God that abides with us into eternity. Jesus says to him, "Today salvation has come to this house, because this man, too, is a son of Abraham. For the Son of Man came to seek and to save the lost."

God's grace is a gift that is meant to be shared. When God's grace is honestly received in a person's heart, mind, and soul, it reveals to us his living grace. God's grace has been alive and functioning in the world since the creation of the world. God's living grace leads the people of Israel out of exile and bondage in Egypt to the promised land (Exodus 13–14).

God's grace has been with Daniel when he is wrongly accused and thrown in the lion's den.

> So, the king gave the order, and they brought Daniel and threw him into the lions' den. The king said to Daniel, "May your God, whom you serve continually, rescue you!" (Daniel 6:16)

> At the first light of dawn, the king got up and hurried to the lions' den. When he came near the den, he called to Daniel in an anguished voice, "Daniel, servant of the living God, has your God, whom you serve continually, been able to rescue you from the lions?" Daniel answered, "May the king live forever! My God sent his angel, and he shut the mouths of the lions. They have not hurt me, because I was found innocent in his sight. Nor have I ever done any wrong before you, Your Majesty." The king was overjoyed and gave orders to lift Daniel out of the den. And when Daniel

was lifted from the den, no wound was found on him, because he had trusted in his God. (Daniel 6:19–23)

When examples of God's living grace are witnessed, his grace comes alive in the people who witness it. The king knows he has been tricked into making a law that hurts Daniel, whom he is fond of. Daniel's enemies want him destroyed. And when the king learns Daniel is safe, he knows that God has spared Daniel, and he also feels blessed. And God's living grace works in the heart of king also.

I witness God's living grace in a nine-year-old boy when he approaches me and asks, "Pastor, can we talk." He asks, "Will you baptize me. I know that is what God wants."

I agree with him, and he wants to be baptized as soon as possible. And we go to his parents, and I am sure they know what their son and I have talked about. They are happy and want to know what they need to plan. The boy's extended family is present for the baptism. And the living grace of God is so present as you see the love between the boy and his family. The boy asks me, "How soon can I read the Bible for church?" He reads the following week, and his grandparents start attending the church and eventually become members.

The living grace of God has the power over people, families, and the whole world. This has occurred during the years of ministry in Pennsylvania. The sad but holy part of this life story is, after I developed a relationship with the grandparents, the grandfather is diagnosed with cancer, and he has had a surgery and treatments. He and I develop a deep friendship on this end-life journey. There are many times that I feel ill-equipped to say the right thing, and those are the times the Holy Spirit, through living grace, speaks through me or keeps me quiet.

The living grace of God ushers my friend to his eternal home. I officiate the memorial service and offer support through their grief. And this leads to all of their children and more grandchildren coming to faith in Christ Jesus. And remember, it all has started from a nine-year-old boy asking to be baptized. We never underestimate the living grace of God working for us and working in us.

John Wesley taught that "God's grace is unearned and that we were not to be idle waiting to experience grace but we are to engage in the means of grace. The means of grace are ways God works invisibly in disciples, hastening, strengthening; and confirming faith so that God's grace pervades in and through disciples. As we look at the means of grace today, they can be divided into works of piety and the works of mercy" (Zondervan Practical Divinity).

The means of grace is a spiritual arena where God uses his disciples (you and me) to help others in times of need and to make more disciples. The important part of this is to remember that it is not our works, but it is God working through us.

There is a dilemma that plagues our society. It is being entitled or rewarded for our actions and works. As a child, I have learned quickly that good behavior and obeying my parents offers me rewards. Therefore, it has been my endeavor to get all the rewards I could get. I don't care about my siblings' rewards. After all, it is all about me. I have learned self-centeredness at an early age, and I don't think it has been my parents' intention to teach me the reward system.

As I grow, the dilemma remains with me in various ways. And then when it comes to growing in faith as a disciple, the residue of the reward system is making my mind confused about grace and service. I am easily moving into the frame of mind that if I do what I think God wants, I am going to be rewarded. I totally miss the point that God has already awarded me eternal life through Christ Jesus. My service now has become a cooperate endeavor between me and God the Father, the Son, and the Holy Spirit. It has taken me a little while to learn God is much smarter and more gracious than me.

> I am the vine; you are the branches. If you remain in me and I in you, you will bear much fruit; apart from me you can do nothing. If you do not remain in me, you are like a branch that is thrown away and withers; such branches are picked up, thrown into the fire and burned. If you remain in me and my words remain in you, ask whatever you wish, and it will be done for

> you. This is to my Father's glory, that you bear much fruit, showing yourselves to be my disciples. (John 15:5–8)

It is God's grace that opens this opportunity for us all. And with God's perfecting grace at work in us, we can become more than we can ever imagined.

The scripture on the previous page teaches another aspect of God's grace. It is the grace that disciplines and warns us as needed. The part of the text that warns is "If you do not remain in me, you are like a branch that is thrown away and withers; such branches are picked up, thrown into the fire and burned." Living grace leaves the image of God upon us. It is only the image of God that places an eternal image upon us. Love and grace are the reasons God wants us to be the best we can be.

And if all these are enough grace for all people, Jesus says, "If you remain in me and my words remain in you, ask whatever you wish, and it will be done for you." By grace, we are opened up to a relationship with God; by grace, we are taught and challenged; and by grace, we are given the chance to ask God for anything. As we grow in this relationship with God, we learn what to ask for, and our character learns to seek the will of God.

"This is to my Father's glory, that you bear much fruit, showing yourselves to be my disciples." God's grace fulfills in us his will and commands. Many generations of religious people live under the idea that we earn our way to God and eternal life. God works through us in order to manifest in us the glory he desires. God does not expect us to do what we cannot do. Jesus teaches us—"Follow Me"—and he will make your life honoring for God and beneficial for you.

> The law was brought in so that the trespass might increase. But where sin increased, grace increased all the more, so that, just as sin reigned in death, so also grace might reign through righteousness to bring eternal life through Jesus Christ our Lord. (Romans 5:20–21)

The Apostle Paul teaches us that God grace is the reigning power of God. When corruption and chaos try to rule the day, grace has the power to defeat corruption and chaos and produce the righteous power of God. In our theologies, we seem to teach that grace is only the unmerited favor of God.

When we look at God's grace as unmerited favor, like a holy blanket or an invisible force field, we do God a disservice, and we limit ourselves. The grace of God is mightier than all our resistance. It will eventually reign in the heart of all people.

> Like the rest, we were by nature deserving of wrath. But because of his great love for us, God, who is rich in mercy, made us alive with Christ even when we were dead in transgressions—it is by grace you have been saved. And God raised us up with Christ and seated us with him in the heavenly realms in Christ Jesus, in order that in the coming ages he might show the incomparable riches of his grace, expressed in his kindness to us in Christ Jesus. For it is by grace you have been saved, through faith—and this is not from yourselves, it is the gift of God—not by works, so that no one can boast. For we are God's handiwork, created in Christ Jesus to do good works, which God prepared in advance for us to do. (Ephesians 2:3–10)

The Apostle Paul teaches the church in Ephesus that we are saved by grace. The corruption that is part of the world is due to the sin that started in the Garden of Eden. That sin has changed the nature of humans to such a degree that humanity has become willing to separate from God. The results of separation from God leads to wrath and eternal death. "But because of his great love for us, God, who is rich in mercy, made us alive with Christ even when we were dead in transgressions—it is by grace you have been saved." Grace produces the opportunity for the "but" in the above verse. Grace has taken on wrath and won.

The great love and mercy of God is revealed to the world through grace. It is often said that the "but" in a sentence changes the direction of a situation. It clearly does in this one. The condition of wrath is transformed by grace. The grace of God also produces faith in the heart of his people—"For it is by grace you have been saved, through faith."

> If any of you lacks wisdom, you should ask God, who gives generously to all without finding fault, and it will be given to you. But when you ask, you must believe and not doubt, because the one who doubts is like a wave of the sea, blown and tossed by the wind. (James 1:5–6)

The verse above will lead my audience into a new perspective about grace. And I will bring an end to this chapter of the multiple aspects of grace in the next couple of pages. If in the future there are people who want to know more than this book offers on the multiple aspects of God's grace—for instance, what happens in heaven when we get there—those are pages I am willing to share to those willing to read.

The above text is a letter to the church in Jerusalem and more from the half-brother of Jesus, James. The gospel of John 7 relates the disbelieving character of all Jesus's half-brothers. Nevertheless, Jesus continues his ministry, and at the foot of the cross where Jesus surrenders his life for the world, James, Jude and the others accepts that Jesus is God in the flesh.

The point here is that James is a perfect example of a doubter. And he is sharing with his audience a valuable piece of information. If you are a doubter, then you can ask God for the wisdom to sort out what is truth and what is false. James believes in a false law system and, consequently for a period of time, does not believe his half-brother Jesus, who is the Messiah. And then the true wisdom of God is poured out on him through the Holy Spirit. He asks God, "Give me wisdom," and in the moment, it arrives. Wisdom comes by the grace of God.

As a pastor and chaplain, there are many times when I feel I am in over my head. If you don't know that saying, in other words, I feel unsure of myself in the moment. I have prayed "God give me wisdom when I need it" early in my ministry. And I have prayed that same prayer probably a thousand times. And that is due to the point that each life circumstance is different.

As a chaplain involved with a medical team, I meet a patient who is diagnosed with a terminal heart condition. The patient is frail, weights about ninety pounds. She is a person of faith, and it has been challenged due to her health condition and the lack of interest in her from the church she has attended for years. I remember one of her first questions to me was, What have I done wrong? I am a very experienced spiritual counselor, but I have no words in the moment. Her husband is there. We put our arms around each other, and I say, "God and I will get you through this."

There is no textbook that prepares a pastor/chaplain for this moment. It's the grace of God working and loving through you. This is the beginning of a deep pastoral relationship with the wife and spouse. The patient stabilizes and is considered not in need of the medical services this team provides. And during this consideration, her husband develops a serious condition and is in need of surgery. It is that time when the spouse and patient need support, and I encourage the team to continue to support her in this challenging time.

It is important to remember medical teams are great, yet they function under certain rules and regulations. God's grace does not always have a place to function in our culture. Fortunately, I am in a role that dwells between the spiritual and emotional of the culture. I convince the team to continue support for this family due to the extenuating circumstances, and it works out.

I share this with you hoping you get the idea of the broad power of the grace of God. It not only functions for a person to come to faith in Christ Jesus. The grace of God is like a presence that we don't control; we only experience it. I can share this final word about the grace of God. It is vast, and I don't think multiple grace is adequate to define it. I can only tell you that through God's grace with Christ Jesus, we are saved and transformed.

CHAPTER 11

All Aboard

The true light that gives light to everyone was coming into the world. He was in the world, and though the world was made through him, the world did not recognize him. He came to that which was his own, but his own did not receive him. Yet to all who did receive him, to those who believed in his name, he gave the right to become children of God—children born not of natural descent, nor of human decision or a husband's will, but born of God. The Word became flesh and made his dwelling among us. We have seen his glory, the glory of the one and only Son, who came from the Father, full of grace and truth. (John 1:9–14)

The text and title for this chapter have to do with making a lasting commitment to a relationship with God. *All aboard* are the words that a ticket master of a train and possibly a bus driver say to customers taking a journey. I remember the few times I have ridden a train and hearing these words. The point from a spiritual perspective is, Have we jumped on the glory train that leads to heaven and eternal life? At least two matters will occur in this chapter: one, for the person not onboard, you are missing an opportunity of an eternal lifetime, and two, for the person who is onboard, you are in for the ride of your eternal lifetime.

The text is sharing with the world the nature of Christ Jesus. Christ Jesus is the Word. We learn from Genesis 1 that God speaks and creation comes into being, and it is good. There is then and still is a physical and spiritual presence of God. Jesus is the physical presence of God. And the Holy Spirit is then the spiritual presence of God. Therefore, when God speaks, Jesus is the physical presence that accomplishes the words of God. The unseen God then reveals himself in Christ Jesus. The creator of all things is willing to step into that which he created in order to redeem the world and reveal himself to everyone who will believe. Are you all aboard? Are you on the glory train? Your ticket has been paid for by the lord and savior Christ Jesus.

"All Aboard" is about moving from the worldly perspective of faith and religion and moving toward the heavenly perspective of faith and godliness. Jesus uses the phrase "the kingdom of God is like" or "the kingdom of heaven is like" in several parables to illustrate the nature of God's kingdom. However, the exact number of times Jesus has used this phrase is not clear. According to some sources, the phrase "kingdom of God" appears fifty-three times in the New Testament gospels, almost always on the lips of Jesus. Other sources (like Biblehub.com) suggest that the phrase appears fourteen times in Mark, thirty-one times in Luke, and thirty-two times in Matthew.

There comes a time in a believer's life when they feel the real presence of Christ Jesus via the Holy Spirit. When that occurs for me, my mindset goes from thinking only worldly thoughts and principals to the influence of heavenly thinking. In other words, the will of God becomes more important than my will or the influence of the world. This is a gradual process. What occurs is that the character of God gradually gives you opportunities to look at life situations in a new and compassionate way. John the Baptist has had this new life image of Jesus.

> The next day John saw Jesus coming toward him and said, "Look, the Lamb of God, who takes

away the sin of the world! This is the one I meant when I said, 'A man who comes after me has surpassed me because he was before me.' I myself did not know him, but the reason I came baptizing with water was that he might be revealed to Israel. Then John gave this testimony: "I saw the Spirit come down from heaven as a dove and remain on him. And I myself did not know him, but the one who sent me to baptize with water told me, 'The man on whom you see the Spirit come down and remain is the one who will baptize with the Holy Spirit.' I have seen and I testify that this is God's Chosen One." John the Baptist said, "Look, the Lamb of God, who takes away the sin of the world!" (John 1:29–34)

Do you see yourself as someone who does not have this type of perception of Jesus? Are you willing to give yourself the excuse to say "I was not there then." I remind you, Jesus is the God who was, who is, and who is to come. Jesus speaks inspirations to all generations. Jesus often says, "He who has ears, let them here what the spirit says to the churches." Revelation 3 is one of those places. Jesus and the Holy Spirit are by no means done speaking to this generations of believers.

I want you to be all aboard so that like John the Baptist, you know when the spirit of Christ Jesus is with you. The reason I say this is due to the many ministry opportunities I have experienced as a pastor and chaplain. I believe in the vast power of Christ Jesus, and I have experienced it firsthand. A dear friend Lynn, who is a patient while I am serving as a chaplain, has felt the presence of Jesus and she does not know how to respond. She has experienced a broad perspective of religious teachings. Nevertheless, the Holy Spirit begins revealing to her the real presence of Jesus. We talk about the character of Jesus that God uses as an inspiration and example for our lives. Some people accept the words of Jesus as an inspiration, but some with doubt. Jesus says, "Come to Me, I am gentle and humble at heart" (Matthew 11:28).

This is not up for debate. We cannot gauge the heart of Jesus, God in the flesh. What the options are is to receive and follow the character of Jesus or die in hell. Being all aboard is not about us just waiting for the glory train to come and pick us up and take you to heaven, but it is about accepting the character of Jesus as the benchmark. And when we do that, our seat on the glory train is secured. There is a complication about this endeavor: we still live in this world, and Satan is going to challenge every child of God. He has tempted Jesus and lost (Matthew 4). The important part is, What do we do when the challenge arrives?

> The sea was getting rougher and rougher. So, they asked him, "What should we do to you to make the sea calm down for us?" "Pick me up and throw me into the sea," he replied, "and it will become calm. I know that it is my fault that this great storm has come upon you." Instead, the men did their best to row back to land. But they could not, for the sea grew even wilder than before. Then they cried out to the LORD, "Please, LORD, do not let us die for taking this man's life. Do not hold us accountable for killing an innocent man, for you, LORD, have done as you pleased." Then they took Jonah and threw him overboard, and the raging sea grew calm. At this the men greatly feared the LORD, and they offered a sacrifice to the LORD and made vows to Him. (Jonah 1:11–16)

I repeat the above text now as a reminder of the escape attempt of Jonah. Jonah is requested by God to preach to the people of Nineveh. Jonah doesn't like the people of Nineveh and feels it is possible to run away from God. That doesn't work for Jonah, and he fulfills the will of God eventually. Who is affected when you run from God? The people of Nineveh repents and are spared from God's wrath. That is what Jonah's preaching accomplished.

Being all aboard considers the other people on the ship that are struggling. In this text, there is one person who takes a selfish attitude, and it jeopardizes the lives of others. When we accept what we want over the articles of created truth for humanity, then we jeopardize all humanity. Is that fair, right, or good, or holy? No! Men are men, and women are women. It is not right to jeopardize our culture with gender indiscretions. When we accept the "all aboard" gift, we need to take into consideration the others on the train. It is totally inappropriate to cast our sinful behavior on another faithful passenger. And yet there are a lot of people willing to criticize and even persecute Christians for their faith in one man and one woman created by God.

Jonah 1 says, "Then they took Jonah and threw him overboard, and the raging sea grew calm." God and moms are always telling their children who not to hang out with. In the case of Jonah, God wants him thrown overboard to prove to the people that the storm is in the hand of God, Jonah, and the other passengers too. Moms want their children to have good friends that will be good for their children and keep them out of trouble. God wants to share salvation to the world. God first saves the people on the ship by stopping Jonah's sin. Then the people of Nineveh are saved when they respond to the word of God spoken through Jonah and they repent.

Jonah, like many people, is shortsighted. He doesn't want to consider the bigger picture, the work of God for all people through people. The prophetic part of this story is, Jesus is called to do what Jonah does not want to do. Jesus does it for a world full of sinful people. The major difference between Jonah and Jesus is that Jesus is the Messiah, the savior of the world. Three days and three nights in the belly of a fish and three days until the resurrection of Jesus is not a coincidence. People are informed well in advance that the Messiah will arrive, preach the word of God, take the sins of the world, and rise again.

There is over two thousand years of the gospel story that Jesus is the Messiah. He arrives to accomplish the work of God. And that is to give salvation to all who will believe in God the Father, the Son, and the Holy Spirit. And this prophetic message will not end. Christ Jesus will one day return and cleanse the world of sin and redeem all creation. It would be easy to criticize Jonah for his disobeying God, but then what about me and the rest of the world? The story of Jonah tells us of how inadequate he feels for the job of saving God's people. So much so that he runs from the task. Most people would do the same. There is only one who gets on board with us, calms our seas, heals our moments, and reveals the way to eternal life: Christ Jesus.

> For through the law I died to the law so that I might live for God. I have been crucified with Christ and I no longer live, but Christ lives in me. The life I now live in the body, I live by faith in the Son of God, who loved me and gave Himself for me. (Galatians 2:19–20)

Again, I share these words of the Apostle Paul. I use an Old Testament text Jonah as a revelation of the forthcoming work of Christ Jesus. Now I want to share with you the work of God in the Apostle Paul. The point is that before Jesus came in the flesh, he has been giving the world clues of his character and ministry to come. And now that He has arrived in the hearts and lives of people, his ministry continues. The apostle is all aboard, are you?

The "all aboard" spirit is also a gift of God's grace. The Apostle Paul accepts this spiritual gift and says, "The life I now live in the body, I live by faith in the Son of God, who loved me and gave Himself for me. I no longer live, but Christ lives in me." There is room in everyone's heart and soul for the presence and spirit of God to live. Rev. Billy Graham says, "There is a God shaped vacuum in everyone, that only God can fill." All aboard challenges us to pursue God, the Holy Spirit.

The reason the Apostle Paul can say "Christ lives in me" is via the power of the Holy Spirit. Jesus's physical presence on earth has some limitations, such as he cannot be in more than one place at a time physically. But that does not mean that Jesus is not spiritually omniscient. The Trinity is in constant connection. What Jesus shows the world is that when humankind is all aboard with God, miracles occur. Jesus sent out seventy-two disciples to heal, cast out demons, and teach the day of the Lord's favor. They are all aboard, and they are amazed at what has happened in their lives and ministries. Luke 10:17 (NIV) says, "The seventy-two returned with joy and said, 'Even the demons submit to us in your name.'"

There are many amazing stories that have occurred when people are all aboard with Christ Jesus. Tony Campolo tells a story of a Jewish boy who suffers under the Nazis during World War II. (We must never forget Jesus is a Jewish boy too.) The little boy and his family are gunned down by Nazis SS troops. Amazingly, the little boy is not hit by the bullets and pretends he is dead. They are covered in a shallow grave, and after nightfall, the boy dugs himself free. He goes from house to house in the town seeking help, but everyone turns him down.

Then he arrives at a house, and in the moment when the lady of the family opens the door to see him, the Spirit speaks through him, and he says, "Don't you recognize me? I am Jesus, the one you say you love." The woman sweeps him into her arms and kisses him. They take the boy into their home and cares for him as their own child. (This is from Charles Swindoll's book of stories and illustrations.) All aboard has the spiritual power to act in the moment and unite people in such a way that it can only be defined as a miracle.

An outrageous part of human interaction is separation and classes. People are separated from God through the sin that has occurred in the Garden of Eden. Christ Jesus comes into the world and remedies the separation from God by taking the sins of the world on his righteous body. So if God the Father, the Son, and the Holy Spirit remedy the separation from God, how can we imagine that humanity being separated is okay with God? The point here is, all aboard with God also needs to be worked out as unity in humanity.

> How good and pleasant it is when God's people live together in unity! It is like precious oil poured on the head, running down on the beard,

> running down on Aaron's beard, down on the collar of his robe. It is as if the dew of Hermon were falling on Mount Zion. For there the LORD bestows His blessing, even life forevermore. (Psalm 133:1–3 NLT)

The Old Testament Psalm on the previous page does not leave too much room for interpretation of "How pleasant it is when God's people live in unity." This is the spiritual nature of God's people. All aboard means just what it says to all.

> On that very day Noah and his sons, Shem, Ham and Japheth, together with his wife and the wives of his three sons, entered the ark. They had with them every wild animal according to its kind, all livestock according to their kinds, every creature that moves along the ground according to its kind and every bird according to its kind, everything with wings. Pairs of all creatures that have the breath of life in them came to Noah and entered the ark. The animals going in were male and female of every living thing, as God had commanded Noah. Then the LORD shut him in. (Genesis 7:13–16)

The circumstances of Noah, his family, and the earthly creatures are a one-time action of God to clean up the mess that humanity makes for itself. And should any of us question why we need a righteous savior to take away the sins of the world? Nevertheless, in this amazing circumstance of Noah, his family, and the animals male and female, there is unity. For forty days and nights, they live together in unity. Anyone can imagine their own ideas for this text. Anyone can challenge or attempt to spin their own ideas for this text. It has been done and probably will be done again. Set all that aside; if you have ears, hear what the Spirit says to the world: unite in Chris Jesus and be all aboard.

If you can imagine your own ideas regarding this text and whether you like it or believe it, then all aboard requires that you listen to the ideas of deep faith and even more so the will of God. People of deep faith recognize this story as a moment when God has chosen to break his own heart and clear the land of sin. Satan has tricked the people into corruption. God has cleansed it up.

The Genesis text reveals to the world that God removes the people created in his image from the pit of corruption and washes away their sins. It is presumptuous for all other generations to think that God washes the earth clean and doesn't take the cleansed ones to himself. We don't tell God what to do. All aboard calls you to pray about that situation, even though it has been a thousands of years ago. They are created in the image of God too.

> Hearing that Jesus had silenced the Sadducees, the Pharisees got together. One of them, an expert in the law, tested him with this question: "Teacher, which is the greatest commandment in the Law?" Jesus replied: "'Love the Lord your God with all your heart and with all your soul and with all your mind.' This is the first and greatest commandment. And the second is like it: 'Love your neighbor as yourself.' All the Law and the Prophets hang on these two commandments. (Matthew 22:34–40)

In the New Testament, we find the power of God working to unify. Even in this moment of challenge from the Sadducees and Pharisees, Jesus does not condemn them, but he teaches them. He uses words from their scriptures and laws to clarify the character of God. And the Trinity reveals to us that God's character is unity. It is easy to see that some of the Sadducees and Pharisees are not all aboard. And the reason they are not all aboard is not due to the power of Jesus, but it is due to their personal, religious, and cultural agendas.

As a pastor and chaplain, I have met many people in my ministry who allow their personal agendas to distance them from God. For example, during the COVID-19 pandemic, I have been one of the few chaplains that is allowed in hospitals and retirement facilities. I have been willing to wear the appropriate protective equipment. I have been tested regularly, and I have been given the vaccines. In these facilities, there are patients and residents who have not seen a clergy person for months.

Consequently, many church people have not received the sacraments for months. I am very familiar with sacraments procedures with all Christian faiths. Therefore, I have been willing to take the sacraments to all the people. On a few occasions, some of the people refuses to receive them from me because I am not their particular priest. And the outrageous part of it is, I am blessed by so many priests, pastors, and bishops to administer these sacraments because they cannot. The point here is that some people, like Sadducees and Pharisees, cannot see the work of God standing right in front of them. They never unite their heart and soul to God the Father, the Son, and the Holy Spirit.

Some people think they are all aboard with God but then resist the work and will of God happening around them. Now hear me clearly in this matter. I am not suggesting people to abandon their lifelong faith tradition, nor am I suggesting that people run after any flamboyant speaker. I am telling people to know their faith and unity with God, and the false teachers will stick out like a sore thumb. If your faith tradition does not lead you to the heart of God, then I would strongly suggest you find out why.

Are you happy with dropping your kids off for two hours and engaging into a religious concert and calling it worship and time with God? Are you happy with going to your somber service of familiar songs and drift somewhere between sleep and lunch and call that worship and time with God? All aboard requires a desire to be in the presence of God during worship and hear the clear gospel of God in Christ Jesus preached. I have preached and taught children, forty-year-olds, and ninety-year-olds, and they all are awake and willing to be with God in the moment. That is *all aboard*! These people feel the real unity of God and one another. They marvel, share, and feel they are in the presence of God.

How can I, as your author, get you all aboard? I don't, and I can't. And yet I know the Lord and Christ Jesus in such a personal way that I can assure you that He can.

> When Jesus came to the region of Caesarea Philippi, he asked his disciples, "Who do people say the Son of Man is?" They replied, "Some say John the Baptist; others say Elijah; and still others, Jeremiah or one of the prophets." "But what about you?" He asked. "Who do you say I am?" Simon Peter answered, "You are the Messiah, the Son of the living God." Jesus replied, "Blessed are you, Simon son of Jonah, for this was not revealed to you by flesh and blood, but by my Father in heaven. And I tell you that you are Peter, and on this rock I will build my church, and the gates of Hades will not overcome it. I will give you the keys of the kingdom of heaven; whatever you bind on earth will be bound in heaven, and whatever you loose on earth will be loosed in heaven." Then he ordered his disciples not to tell anyone that he was the Messiah. (Matthew 16:13–20)

This text is a holy moment. Jesus knows his disciples are getting deeper into the spiritual arena with him. They ask him to teach them how to pray (Matthew 6). They receive their spiritual gifts from him (Luke 10). And it has come to the time for Jesus to give them the opportunity to say what is bubbling up in their hearts and souls. I challenge you to get this close to Jesus; I am there in awe and humility. Peter, without hesitation, says what is in his heart and soul. "You are the Messiah, the son of the living god."

Jesus's response is the holy part. "Blessed are you, Simon, son of Jonah, for this was not revealed to you by flesh and blood, but by my Father in heaven." What is holy here is that Jesus knows when God the Father or God the Holy Spirit has rested assurance on a person's heart and soul.

No one can be halfway assured forever. One becomes like Peter, all aboard with Christ Jesus. Or one looks for a sidecar to ride out the "all aboard" journey. If I haven't already said this, *all aboard* is not an option. Jesus paid for the world's ticket, and it is not up for debate. God has called all creation to come home for glory. Get out of any sidecar you are riding and get on board with eternal life offered by God the Father, the Son, and the Holy Spirit.

What is the sidecar? Anything that gets in between you, God, and satisfying the true hunger in your heart and soul. I am a spiritual counselor. I have been given award from the medical teams I have worked with for my ability to get people out of the sidecar and all aboard. What is important to understand is that I am well-trained in Christianity, Judaism, Islam, Buddhism, Hinduism, the magics, and many other forms of spiritual influence. Remember, I live near Sarasota, Florida, the home of the circus.

Therefore, I am not a narrow-focused, uninformed soul. I am a person who—by some holy, glorious gift beyond that which I deserve—have been led into the arenas of the kingdom of God. And in some bigger-than-me way, I am able to reach all people with the eternal love of God. That is why I know *all aboard* is not optional; it is all about the love of God.

> Turn to Me and be saved, all you ends of the earth; for I am God, and there is no other. By myself I have sworn, My mouth has uttered in all integrity a word that will not be revoked: Before Me every knee will bow; by Me every tongue will swear. They will say of Me, "In the LORD alone are deliverance and strength." (Isaiah 45:22–24)

The above scripture is vital for all humanity to understand. Some people may find these words produce anger in their heart, some fear in their heart, and then some with peace and comfort in their heart. For the people of Isaiah's era, they are a comfort.

The people of the era on the previous page are being oppressed by a foreign nation. And the words from God are a comfort because they know God is aware and their oppressor will eventually bow to the power of a righteous god. We can find ourselves in an arena of oppression through our social environment, through our life choices—both good and bad—and by ignoring our spiritual health and development.

For instance, our social environment can have challenges regarding education, work pressures, relationship pressures, and more. One believes education leads to better opportunities, and yet they are competing with many other educated people. Education is great and necessary while not answering every challenge. With work, some employment are secure, and some are not. Some employers are considerate, and some are not. And relationships in an era where entitlement is prevalent and some cases are ramped, oppression seems overwhelming.

The point in this writing is, when a person develops a solid relationship with God, they are better at managing the oppressive moments. For faith in God will remind us that we are a child of God and that nothing is going to reign oppression over you forever. God will use your faith to secure you in hope. God will use his Holy Spirit to bend the knee of the oppressor. Some people like to use phrases like "What goes around comes around." That is never the case.

> You, then, why do you judge your brother or sister? Or why do you treat them with contempt? For we will all stand before God's judgment seat. It is written: "As surely as I live," says the Lord, "every knee will bow before me; every tongue will acknowledge God." So then, each of us will give an account of ourselves to God. Therefore, let us stop passing judgment on one another. Instead, make up your mind not to put any stumbling block or obstacle in the way of a brother or sister. (Romans 14:10–13 NIV)

In the Romans 14 text, we read almost the same words as the Isaiah 45 text. The Apostle Paul goes into detail about the point that God is making to all people of all generations. When a generation, social group, or relationship oppresses others, they are in sin and are forcing their way into arena of the judgement of God. The Romans text is insisting on unity and calling people to get all aboard.

> For the Lord your God is the God of gods and Lord of lords. He is the great God, the mighty and awesome God, who shows no partiality and cannot be bribed. (Deuteronomy 10:17)

The omniscient power of God is able to see and know how to handle all human concerns. God sends the angel Gabriel to many people to quiet their souls and some their mouths, to prepare people for coming action of God, and to set the captives free. Read about Peter in prison from the Book of Acts. I have come to understand at a very personal and faithful level that God is in control, and I am all aboard with letting him guide my life through the Holy Spirit.

It is quite clear that how closely we relate to God the Father, the Son, and the Holy Spirit has an impact on us and the people around us. My dad use to say something like "I can see or smell a con man a mile away." My dad can be a little crass at times; nevertheless, life experience has given him insight into people who are dishonest and disloyal. My dad have not considered himself better than others. He has taught me, "If people cannot trust you, you will go nowhere in life." He has believed in God although was not a church-going, religious person. My point here is that at some level, the Spirit of God has commanded his actions and soul. He has liked Billy Graham, and he has felt he has been honest, and he has liked George Jones because he has felt he has been a good singer and a real man challenged by this crazy world. The amazing and also complicated part of the human experiencing the intersection of heaven and earth is what does he do next.

I am closing this chapter with the point that all aboard has to be all encompassing. In other words, one cannot be all aboard in one area of life with God and then in another area of life jump off the train.

> When they had finished eating, Jesus said to Simon Peter, "Simon son of John, do you love me more than these?" "Yes, Lord," he said, "you know that I love you." Jesus said, "Feed my lambs." Again, Jesus said, "Simon son of John, do you love me?" He answered, "Yes, Lord, you know that I love you." Jesus said, "Take care of my sheep." The third time he said to him, "Simon son of John, do you love me?" Peter was hurt because Jesus asked him the third time, "Do you love me?" He said, "Lord, you know all things; you know that I love you." Jesus said, "Feed my sheep." (John 21:15–17)

The above text is the moment after the resurrection of Jesus when he meets his disciple by the lake fishing. Jesus takes the time to have an important moment with Peter. During the trial of Jesus, Peter denies three times that he is a disciple of Jesus. It is looking bad for Jesus, and Peter is challenged. Jesus knows Peter's love for him and his willingness to die with him, but Peter's death will not serve the cause of Jesus for spreading the word of God. So a spiritual fear comes over Peter to protect him.

The point I want to drive home here is what all aboard means to Jesus is in John 17:15–16, which says, "My prayer is not that you take them out of the world but that you protect them from the evil one. They are not of the world, even as I am not of it." All aboard gives us a new image and residence in heaven with Jesus. When you get onboard with Jesus, the world does not own your eternity. We are a new creation. *All aboard* trusts God with everything. I am calling out, all aboard! Amen.

CHAPTER 12

A Peace of My Mind

Have you ever said, "I sure would like to give them a piece of my mind"? If you are human, I'm sure, at one time or another, you have said this. These words are a byproduct of frustration and struggle. Whether people say it directly to God or to people they are in relationship with, they think it. So let's put this into God and human perspective. If you have thought this, God already knows it. Remember, God is the one who was, who is, and who is to come.

As a chaplain, I have met many frustrated people who have abandoned God the Father, the Son, and the Holy Spirit and invented their own god. And some of those people have made themselves the god of their desire. This is a big problem. Can you save yourself? Therefore, the argument goes on and on.

Let me clue you all into something that is real and important. If you don't already know this, only Christ Jesus saves us. When a person is comfortable with the idea that Christ Jesus has paid the price and opened heaven for us, then self-salvation is foolish. These are the principles of Christian faith. So now let's get real about faith in God. Have you heard the word of God preached? Are you a person that seeks a comfortable place to rest on a Sunday morning, or are you someone who longs to hear what a real relationship with God means?

This is what a peace of my mind is all about. It is surrendering your thoughts and your mind over to the will of God so that you can be more aware of what happens between heaven and earth. Maybe you don't want to know what happens between heaven and earth—shame on you! I have met too many lost and suffering souls who have chosen this pathway. If you are reading this and you are still a skeptic, get your act together! I have helped many people manage the transition from earth to heaven, and my guide has been the holy spirit of God. Giving a peace of my/your mind is about surrendering into the hands of God. And the outcome is heavenly.

> Peter replied "Even if all fall away on account of you, I never will." "I tell you the truth," Jesus answered, "this very night before the roosters crows, you will disown Me three times." But Peter declared, "Even if I have to die with you. I will never disown you." And all the other disciples said the same. (Matthew 26:33–35)

The point of this text is to reveal or remind us of the very uncontrollable circumstances that everyone experiences. Peter is confident that he has peace in his mind, but soon, he finds out differently. I will repeat the play on words regarding this chapter several times. I certainly don't want my audience to think that you are not able to catch on. It is all about establishing a unity with my audience. I have hungered for peace in my life, and one thing I have learned is if you avoid peace in your mind, you will struggle. Believe me, I have struggled.

The Apostle Peter becomes one of the most productive preachers of the New Church movement, according to Acts 2–10 and more. Peter has to become at peace in his mind that at a given moment, he has failed God. Anyone who lives on this earth will have the same feeling at some time, or maybe not. For the maybe-nots, email me, and I will describe the vision of the lake of fire I have once received. There is nothing pleasant about it. In Peter's situation, God knows his heart is pure, and he gives Peter the chance to prove it. In John 21, Jesus says, "Feed my sheep."

If there is ever going to be a chance for you to offer to God a peace in your mind, it means having a relationship with Christ Jesus and knowing he loves you. Let me explain. A peace of my mind is not always getting my prayers answered the way I want. It does not mean that all my yard work is miraculously done. What it means is that in the most human moments of my life, God calls me out to learn his will. Several times a week, I am called out of my comfort zone and on to my knees to learn from the rich graces of God.

There is a subject that needs to be dwelt with in this matter. We read how Peter denies Jesus, and if you have read the New Testament account, you should have read the part of the gospel according to Matthew 26:75 (NIV), which says, "Then Peter remembered the word of Jesus had spoken: 'before the rooster crows, you will disown Me three times.' And he went outside and wept bitterly.'" Peter does not have a peace of mind in this moment. Although in John 21, when Jesus reinstates Peter, a peace of my mind is with Peter.

Do you get the idea that Jesus never stops thinking about Peter and, after the resurrection, shows his risen self to the disciples? And this revelation is not just a moment to show a miracle, but it is a moment of spiritual counsel for Peter and the others. Ready or not, your time is coming too. I suggest you get yourself ready for the most glorious human and spiritual experience you will ever have. The world has drifted away from the truth and character of Jesus, and yet he has not drifted away from us. This is a physical, emotional, and spiritual renewal that God the Father, the Son, and the Holy Spirit have been planning to win forever.

Referring back to my experience as a pastor/chaplain, I have met a lot of people who are in limbo about their belief in God and anything spiritual. Let me give you all the ideas and percentages that may clarify my experience. As a pastor, 40 percent of the people in the church are spiritually aware and comfortable with talking about a relationship with God. As a chaplain, 15–20 percent of the people I meet are comfortable talking about a relationship with God. The overwhelming truth in both circumstances is that in crisis or end-of-life situations, people feel the call of God and want to know what to do. Do you get the idea that Jesus never stops thinking about you/us? In both of the cases as pastor and chaplain, I am amazed at the power of God to get people in the place they needed to be for salvation.

Have you gotten the idea yet that a peace of your mind, heart, and soul is what is being sought by God the Father, the Son, and the Holy Spirit? You are not in control of the God who seeks you. There have been many times for me as a pastor that the business of the ministry has led me away from the comfort zone of God. I don't have a job in the mainstream; I have a job in the church. In our current faith battle, we have churches that have become mainstream, and they are nothing more than a business using God as their front. And what everyone needs to know is that we cannot use God. If anyone uses God as a front for fake ministry, then Christ Jesus becomes your judge.

The real subject matter here is that when push becomes to shove in the spiritual realm, what do you want to experience? Do you want to experience the lake of fire that burns with misery for eternity, or do you want eternal bliss? I have seen the lake of fire and can confirm it exists. That is the momentum behind the book's message. God reveals to his messengers pieces of information through dreams or revelation, and they are called to lead us into a right relationship with him.

Friends, I am here as a spokesman for God. I do not have a personal agenda about theology or church policy. I am writing for the salvation of God's people and to encourage the true inspiration of God. It is not I who writes; it is the Christ who writes and lives in me. With that said, I want to share with you all the purpose and character of Christ Jesus.

The purpose of Christ Jesus is to remove my sins, your sins, and the sins of the world. He has accomplished that on the cross where he has been crucified. He is innocent, as Pilate has said, which makes him the only one who can save the world. You may be able to grasp the idea of such a sacrifice for the world or not; nevertheless, it is finished. The purpose of Christ Jesus can be challenging to perceive. Remember, he is God in the flesh, and we are not.

Jesus's purpose is called justification. That means what the law requires for humanity he accomplishes for the world on the cross. And then after the resurrection, he breathes his spirit upon us, and that is called sanctification. God's work for us is God's work in us.

The big question to Jesus is, Why would you do this for me? The simplest answer to these questions is this: we are not in the Garden of Eden when the first sin has entered human existence. No, I am not saying that if I have the same experience as Adam that I would have resisted the temptation.

What I am saying is that even though sin has entered the human experience in the Garden of Eden, God does not hold us responsible for their actions. God provides a way, in Christ Jesus, to redeem all humanity from the original sin. You might ask, What has this to do with peace in my mind? Learn this, the tabernacle, the temple, the synagogue, and the church are structured to teach us that God is leading us back to the Garden of Eden. What this means is that we all can learn how intimate and precious are the moments that God has created for Adam and Eve and you and me. Sin has not won the day; redemption in Christ Jesus wins the day. Our minds need a place to rest with peace. Only in the mind is there intersection with the spirit of God, a place of peace that exist through the holiness of God.

The gospel according to John focuses on an up-close and personal and intimate relationship with Jesus. This disciple John is fascinated with Jesus. He is young enough not to have developed harmful skepticisms, even though he was a Jew known by the religious leaders of the day. John witnesses the miraculous power of God that reveals in the hand and ministry of Christ Jesus. He also witnesses the lovingkindness part of God that is revealed through Christ Jesus. He watches as Jesus heals, casts out demons, feeds thousands, walks on the water, and allows him to rest in his presence upon his shoulder.

> My prayer is not for them alone. I pray also for those who will believe in me through their message, that all of them may be one, Father, just as you are in me and I am in you. May they also be in us so that the world may believe that you have sent me. I have given them the glory that you gave me, that they may be one as we are one. I in them and you in me—so that they may be brought to complete unity. Then the world will

> know that you sent me and have loved them even as you have loved me." "Father, I want those you have given me to be with me where I am, and to see my glory, the glory you have given me because you loved me before the creation of the world."
> (John 17:20–24 NIV)

The witness of the disciple of John is this: if you are willing to get over yourself and the lies of the world, you can know Christ Jesus as a brother, lord, and savior. Getting over yourself means not needing to be in charge of everything, including Jesus. Those who put themselves in charge of Jesus have lost their opportunity to go with the risen Messiah. The text above are the words of Jesus that only disciple John feels is important for the world to hear.

The scripture above are the words of Jesus for all of us who decide to believe. Here is a little lesson on deciding to believe sooner rather than later. The disciple John decides to believe early on and doesn't look back. He stays by Jesus's side right up to the cross. And on the cross, Jesus asks him to take care of his mother, Mary. And John does. It is a relationship of unity and trust. This relationship is an example for all of us to accept as achievable. The reason that this is achievable for the disciple John is because of love and the Holy Spirit.

"Father, I want those you have given me to be with me where I am, and to see my glory, the glory you have given me because you loved me before the creation of the world." If you think you can't love Jesus like John, you are mistaken. This is a teaching moment.

> I have seen the burden God has laid on the human race. He has made everything beautiful in its time. He has also set eternity in the human heart; yet no one can fathom what God has done from beginning to end. I know that there is nothing better for people than to be happy and to do good while they live. (Ecclesiastes 3:10–12)

I am sharing this scripture again with my audience in hopes that, as we are nearing the end of this book, your heart, soul, and mind may have grown just a little. In this time of my life, I have enjoyed spiritual experiences with God the Father, the Son, and the Holy Spirit, which are second to none. I will admit I have not ridden a chariot of fire, I have not seen a burning bush, and I have not asked Jesus to call me out of the boat to walk on water. And yet I know Jesus so well that I have laid my head on his lap and have been blessed. A peace of your mind is a place and not anything else. There is a peace in my mind that is on the lap of Christ Jesus. It is what he now owns of me, along with my heart and soul. My mind is in God's hand to shape.

Solomon sees this as a burden placed upon humanity. It is a burden in his eyes because he doesn't see the righteousness of Christ Jesus. As a chaplain, I have met hundreds of people who sense the spiritual environment as a burden. The problem is, they don't seek beyond their limited view due to life, work, family, and many other excuses. So when we are willing to go further than Solomon's point of view and accept that God is graciously waiting for us to find him, the peace of our minds he claims forever.

"I know that there is nothing better for people than to be happy and to do good while they live." Remember, this is not your spiritual journey; these are Solomon's words of frustration. Get to know the character of Jesus so intimately through the Gospels that you will know when he walks through your locked doors into your life and shows himself to give you as Spirit and peace.

In John 10:10 (NIV), it says, "The thief comes only to steal and kill and destroy; I have come that they may have life, and have it to the fullest."

These words of Jesus are focused on his love for people. In this text, he says, "I am the Good Shepard; my sheep hear my voice and they follow me." This is an analogy/parable giving us insight into the ability of Jesus to know the character of people. I'm sure there are many powerful, self-serving people in our world who are insulted to think they are like sheep. The fact of the matter is, I have been a chaplain for hundreds who thought they had the world and future in the palm of their hands. To think of themselves as lowly sheep is outrageous.

The point that many of these people fail to understand for the majority of their lives is that Jesus knows what is in the heart, soul, and emotion of all people. "He who has an ear, let him hear what the Spirit says to the churches." In Revelation 3:6, Jesus says this to the world to let us know we need to stop and listen. Everyone needs to admit when it comes to eternal life and our future in heaven and our imminent future, we are like sheep needing a shepherd. For most people, their insight into heaven or their future is limited or nonexistent. For people who truly seek the Lord and Christ Jesus, they will get glimpses of heaven once or twice or many times. Their vision for the future also depends upon on their faith and love for Jesus.

I am going to repeat this text from an earlier chapter because my audience may need to hear it again. In John 1: 50–51 Jesus says, "You believe because I told you I saw you under the fig tree. You will see greater things than that." He then adds, "Very truly I tell you, you will see 'heaven open, and the angels of God ascending and descending on' the Son of Man."

Jesus is talking to Nathanael, who is astonished by the insights of Jesus about his life and his future. Jesus adds, "You will see angels and heaven because of me."

Nathanael stops questioning the insight of Jesus and "then Nathanael declared, 'Rabbi, you are the Son of God; you are the king of Israel.'" Nathanael thinks he is an Israelite with good insight and standing in the culture. When he realizes his insight is limited, Jesus says, "You will see greater things." This is what it means to become a sheep before the shepherd. I don't care how rich or important people become in their life experiences; they all remember a time when they are not in charge and needed others. There maybe a few in this world who will arrogantly say, "I never had to listen to anybody." Let me inform you now, when you come to the end of your life on earth, that attitude will not exist. You will want someone to lead you to the way of eternal life and peace of mind.

I want to share with my audience an experience as a chaplain. I am scheduled to visit a famous pilot—let me call him Mr. Jones.

When I meet him, I say, "I know all kinds of life situations we can talk about them today, or not." He laughs and says, "Let's keep it light for now." As we get to know each other, he enjoys sharing his life stories, and I enjoy listening. He feels he is skilled and enjoys experiences as a pilot with great political and industrial leaders. He also says to me, "I am Catholic, because my family is. I stopped attending church as soon as I was allowed to." I sat, "I am Protestant, and as a child, I did the same thing." We laugh.

In Mr. Jones's and my life experiences, we do not have the peace in our minds to know what Jesus is about. And if it doesn't seem important to our families at the time, it certainly is not important to us. I am fortunate enough to have the Christian people in my life, and from those people, I have learned to trust Jesus and follow him in service. Mr. Jones is a pilot; I am a spiritual counselor. He never looks for faith; he is Catholic, for whatever that means. It is a journey of going from death to life. I am not challenging the Catholic church; I am challenging the leaders.

> "Lord," Martha said to Jesus, "if you had been here, my brother would not have died. But I know that even now God will give you whatever you ask." Jesus said to her, "Your brother will rise again." Martha answered, "I know he will rise again in the resurrection at the last day." "Jesus said to her, "I am the resurrection and the life. The one who believes in me will live, even though they die; and whoever lives by believing in me will never die. Do you believe this?" (John 11:22–26 NIV)

I share this scripture with Mr. Jones to give him the assurance that this earthly life experience is not the final experience. When we are taught the truth of God revealed in the life of Christ Jesus, miracles occur. In the text, we read the conversation between Martha and Jesus. They are close friends. Jesus loves Martha, Mary, and Lazarus, their brother. And even when they are so close, we read the uncertainty in Martha's words. Jesus is their rabbi (teacher). He has the power and insight to create and transform everything.

> Jesus, once more deeply moved, came to the tomb. It was a cave with a stone laid across the entrance. "Take away the stone," he said. "But, Lord," said Martha, the sister of the dead man, "by this time there is a bad odor, for he has been there four days." Then Jesus said, "Did I not tell you that if you believe, you will see the glory of God?" So, they took away the stone. Then Jesus looked up and said, "Father, I thank you that you have heard me. I knew that you always hear me, but I said this for the benefit of the people standing here, that they may believe that you sent me." "When he had said this, Jesus called in a loud voice, "Lazarus, come out!" The dead man came out, his hands and feet wrapped with strips of linen, and a cloth around his face. Jesus said to them, "Take off the grave clothes and let him go." (John 11:38–44 NIV)

It takes a teacher that knows how to teach the truth. Amen.

In the experience of Lazarus, Martha, and Mary, a peace comes over their minds. Although, I don't imagine their lives from that day forward that everything is peaches and cream. I do know that nothing takes away their peace of mind. They are able know that whatever comes their way, "God is with us."

I am fortunate enough to have good teachers in my life who encourages and helps me to know God the Father, the Son, and the Holy Spirit personally. And the holiness movement that I enjoy by faith in the power of the Holy Spirit revealed to me the true purpose of God for all of his people. I am the teacher that God equips, and that helps me be the teacher that Mr. Jones needs for peace of his mind. Mr. Jones says, "When I'm called, I will be happy to fly away with Jesus." I have been with him when he has taken flight.

Peace of My Mind

In my life moments when I thought I am in love but it is not real love, it is not peaceful. There are jealousies and turmoil. On the other hand, when a person falls in love for real, there is an emotional peace the occurs. And then that is often accompanied by peace of heart. When I have realized my family loved me for real, it has been an emotional and heartfelt peace. The peace of my mind is different. One has to make a deliberate effort to have peace of mind. Many world and life circumstances are ready to challenge the peace of your mind. In order to be healthy for oneself and others, a person needs to learn the practice of a peace of their mind. That means to go to a place of surrender only to God.

I want to share with my audience an unconventional and yet inspirational practice I have learned. I have been encouraged by a spiritual mentor/pastor friend to attend a Benedictine monastery throughout one summer. I agree to try it out. I arrive at the monastery, and there is a bookstore, beautiful gardens to enjoy, and prayer and worship services.

My mentor has notified the monks that he has sent me. Two monks take charge of me. Brother James is my Bible teacher and church history teacher. And Brother Luke is my shepherd. The monastery also cares for about fifty sheep. The sheep wool will be an important part of their income. Therefore, caring for their sheep is like a dairy farmer caring for his/her milking cows. It is the right thing to do and a protection of the investment God has given them.

The interesting part of this experience comes about when Brother Luke says, "Do not pet, feed, or interact with any of the sheep. Do not do anything to coax them to follow you." He says, "You will understand in time." The sheep follow Brother Luke around, and he takes wonderful care of them. The reason is that Brother Luke has a peaceful mind with no issues, which the gentle animals could sense. Brother Luke said to me, "Do not worry about them liking you. Like yourself and enjoy whatever it is you do in their presence."

That is what I do while I put out food for the sheep or clean their pens. I look at the beautiful landscape and feel peaceful. After two weeks, one by one, the sheep comes up to me and rubs against me. We are two gentle beings okay with each other. A peace with the environment has come over my mind, and the sheep can sense it. Then I have more sheep following me than I know what to do with. Has it been the power of God working in me? Yes! And yet the most amazing part is, when I look away from me, I enjoy the peace of my mind abundantly.

> All this I have spoken while still with you. But the Advocate, the Holy Spirit, whom the Father will send in my name, will teach you all things and will remind you of everything I have said to you. Peace, I leave with you; my peace I give you. I do not give to you as the world gives. Do not let your hearts be troubled and do not be afraid. (John 14:25–27 NIV)

By this time in the chapter, my audience would like to give me a piece of their mind. The play on words can be good to some people and not so good to others. There are those moments in the conversations between Jesus and his followers that he speaks in parables. And they ask him, "How do you expect us to understand this? Tell us what it means." That is a disciple giving Jesus a piece of his mind, and then when Jesus interprets it, they are at peace. (Read the parable of the sower in Matthew 13:1–23.)

"Peace, I leave with you; my peace I give you. I do not give to you as the world gives. Do not let your hearts be troubled and do not be afraid." The words I think that are important are "I do not give to you as the world gives." It is not news that the world in not at peace. And because the world is not at peace, it is going to affect our peace of mind.

I have a very close and committed relationship to Jesus the Christ, the Word. And I am aware that I am not the only one. I can't lose my peace in Jesus because it is not based on limits. What happens is that Jesus does not say, "Here you go, I give you a dose of peace to last forever."

Peace means "societal friendship and harmony in the absence of hostility and violence." In a social sense, peace is commonly used to mean a lack of conflict (such as war). Psychological peace (such as peaceful thinking and emotions) is less well-defined yet perhaps a necessary precursor to establishing behavioral peace. Peaceful behavior sometimes results from a peaceful inner disposition. Some have expressed the belief that peace can be initiated with certain <u>inner qualities</u>—such as tranquility, forbearance, respect for others and empathy, compassion, kindness, self-control, courage, moderation, forgiveness, good temper, caution, and perspective—that do not depend upon the uncertainties of daily life.

The reason I shared this Wikipedia page is to state the predicament the world is in regarding peace. It often depends on whether the environment and its people are willing to be at peace with you, me, and all others. Therefore, when I am in a peace dilemma in the people around me, I do not look to Wikipedia. I look to the Scripture and the character of Christ Jesus. My effort in this endeavor for peace is to pray for the people and situation in faith. And then I know that Jesus has given me the peace to be wise and compassionate, and it always works out.

I am taking you all near the home stretch in the concept of peace of my mind. One of the most valuable lessons I have learned is to take my peace back to me. Luke 10: 5–6 (NIV) says, "When you enter a house, first say, 'Peace to this house.' If someone who promotes peace is there, your peace will rest on them; if not, it will return to you."

Jesus already gives the disciples a healing advantage. What we all must realize is that the peace of Christ Jesus has a multiple purpose. First, it gives the disciple the Christlike gentleness to be willing to approach people with the wonderful gift of God. His peace also has the power to influence the seeking stranger, and they may welcome such peace. His peace also has the power to convict the evil soul who will reject any concept of peace. And if those are not enough, the peace of Jesus returns to the sincere giver to ease the hurtful words and actions. When the peace of Christ Jesus returns to the injured giver, a healing process takes over.

When Jesus sends out the disciples in Luke 10, they are not sent out forever. They know when to return and talk to him about the events of the ministries. Some of the events cause them extreme excitement, and others need the healing power of the peace of God. In the same way, every pastor, deacon, and leader for Christ Jesus will have their glory days and their painful days. And sometimes, the only way to reclaim the peace is to empty yourself of the pain.

I'm going to close this chapter and book with a real-life story that has occurred in my life and my family's life as I served as a pastor for a church. I wish it has been a happy story; nevertheless, you will know how the words of Jesus "Peace I leave with you" comes true. I have been serving an active church in southwest Florida, and it is going well. And a superintendent of the denomination asks me to take a struggling church in the center of the state. The story the superintendent shares is that the church has been hurt and divided by a controlling pastor and that they need someone with compassion to help them through.

He also asks me to visit a counselor who has experience with the congregation, and I do. Her first question was, How are you with conflict resolution? We talk about that at length, and many times, she pushes me hard on the issue. I finally ask, "Do I seem a nasty personality to you?"

"No," she says, "I can tell I would want you as my pastor." I thought, *What is she not telling me?*

My wife and I meet with the congregation, and they seem nice, and it works very well for quite a while. I am an upbeat, interactive preacher, and the messages are well-received by all people. I have always been a pain to the people who think the morning message is nap time. Within a few weeks, I hear complaints from one person about the way another person is decorating. I say, "I am not good with decor, and I don't micromanage people. You will have to work it out together." Eventually, that turns into an argument that I am drawn into to solve, like it or not.

By some amazing grace, it is resolved and never to surface again. I am not saying there are not a pile of them that will come after. But what I have learned is, their fighting with one another is their way of life, and it causes a lot of people to leave the church.

The point with this church is that they never receive back the healing peace from Christ Jesus. As a matter of fact, they reject the peace of Christ for worldly judgementalism. And here is the spiritual mystery: when God is working his peace, there are dedicated people, and there are loose, affiliated people. The dedicated people receive back their peace, and the others have hungry ears for the words of the devil. Matthew 4 tells the story of how the devil tries to interfere with Jesus's time with the Father and the Holy Spirit in the wilderness.

Just like the people who chase the disciples away, this church thrives on social judgementalism. For some people, it is a sinful, outrageous desire to want to prove that I am better than someone else. And social judgementalism and the concept have a political name all in itself. Nevertheless, that is the spirit of the leadership of this congregation.

I leave these people to their evil because after three years, it has not been changing. A few of the fighters die, and all I can say is "Lord, have your mercy." I am becoming more known in the community, and a few people say, "We met your pastor. What a nice man." But due to the unfriendly environment, people come and go. Fortunately, the snowbirds know the scenario and put up with the people while they are in Florida.

Then when the money-hungry people begin to complain, I do a little research. The money policies are not being followed, and it is outrageous. I inform the finance committee, and I decide to let them audit the practices. Nearing the end of the third year, I notice a daycare across the street that is overfull, and I approach them with the idea of renting some of the unused space at the church. The church is a city block. The director looks at the available spaces and say, "Yes, we could transform these easily and would be able to take on more children." It is great. She later comes back with some potential income figures, and they are good.

The leadership looks at the proposals, and in that particular moment, I am gold money in their pockets. It is less than a year, and the church is making a substantial income. The community is amazed with all the activity. At the same time, a food, clothing, and finance shelter has damage to their building, and it is not usable. I know the director from the community events, and he asks me, "Is there any available space that we could use for a little while?" I show him a garage area that has an adjoining office, and he says it is great. He makes a rental offer to the leadership, and they accept. Again, there is more income than the church has since their claimed dilemma.

The problems for me are when I approach the leadership with the point that this is not a business for financial gain. Now that we have resources, we really need to be disciples of Jesus and make disciples of Jesus. Their response is, "We are not one of those new-wave churches. We have the people we want, and now we have the income we need to keep it running."

I speak with the superintendent about these issues, and he assures me he has my back. "It's not you. It's them." I then decide I will start a monthly Saturday evening event that invites the community as a time to teach the people how to be disciples without them knowing it. It has music, food, and entertainment. I start with prayer, and the band plays gospel, country, oldies rock, and I get a friend who is a magician. And it flourishes. My wife says to me later that the leaders are arguing over who gets the most time and attention, and she drops out as a musician and singer.

I try to balance everything out for unity's sake, and I repeat, here is the spiritual mystery when God is working His peace—there are dedicated people, and there are loosely affiliated people. The dedicated people receive back their peace, and the others have hungry ears for the words of the devil. The event that proves popular for the church and community comes to a disastrous end.

Now there is a cue between the pastor who says "you people need Jesus" and the leadership that is furious for their actions. They are blaming one another, me as the pastor, and the pastor from ten years ago that they say hurt them so much. They demand the superintendent to fix their upset. The ace card that they have is, there is a family member who is in the church and is a multimillionaire. These are people I visit in the hospital when they are sick, and every aspect of sincere pastoral care is given them.

I again speak with the superintendent about the problems and recommend that he moves me out of the church. He says I have no one to take over now. When I meet with other pastors in our area, I am not encouraged at all. It is often said, "All the bad people go to your church." I stick up for the congregation.

I have been praying for that mystery peace to arrive and give the leaders some distance. I continue to preach encouragement and the truth of the Gospel. Then one Monday morning, my wife and I decide to show up in the office to iron out the problems with the leaders. I want my wife there to verify my words. We are there first, and they are angry. I decide we wait until actual church hours start. The church secretary and her husband, who by then have made himself trustee, arrives. They speak briefly, and he leaves the building. Then he returns, and I say to the two of them, "We need to work out these issues between us."

She says, "My lawyer told me not to talk to you."

I reply, "Why are you talking to a lawyer and not your pastor."

At that, her husband rises to his feet and says, "You better shut your f——g mouth, or you are going to be sorry."

I tell my wife to call 911. The police arrives. The husband has a concealed weapon, and the sheriff takes it. In the meantime, I call the conference security to let them know, and the person confirms to the policeman, "This is the pastor. Remove any violators."

And they have a backup plan. Another leader comes sneaking in the side door, and my wife says to the cop, "Check him too. I think he has a gun." The guns are confiscated, and the second man says, "Pastor, can we talk."

I say, "No. Anyone who acts like you people are not of Christ Jesus. You are following the devil. Get out."

The sheriff asks, "Do you want a restraining order placed against them?" And while all this is happening, I am still on the phone with the conference security person, and she says absolutely. And so it is. The police insists they leave, and the leave shouting threats against my wife, our home, and our family.

When I think of the insults yelled at Christ Jesus before he goes to the cross, I, in some way, feel his pain. The conference security person asks us, "Oh my god, you two are okay?"

Later that day, the superintendent calls and asks me to drop the restraining order against the people. And I ask, "Are you not ready to finally clean up this mess?" The multimillionaire family member threatens to sue the conference unless I drop the charges. And again, money wins over the character of Christ Jesus our lord. He promises me everything if I drop the charges, and consequently, I leave that denomination for good.

From that point on, I am able to show the real me to another church not too far away, but it isn't long before the old church starts trying to hurt the new church. I leave there and start my full-time ministry as a medical team chaplain. And what do you know, only after three years, the company elects me as an honorary employee going above and beyond the call of duty. I start a church with some great Christian leaders and friends. I pray that my audience does not see my sharing as a complaint. I empty a horrible time that would have likely be with me forever. Everyone needs to be vulnerable enough to empty their pain and receive the back to you the peace of Christ.

I have been a pastor and a chaplain for years, and I have had the sympathy to listen to every story that has stolen someone's peace—everything from false doctrines to family matters that are outrageous to fears that I am not good enough. And the key to making peace for the patient is when I can get them to empty the wastebasket of their heart and soul and mind and to know they are loved by God the Father, the Son, and the Holy Spirit.

Believe you me, I have heard some stories that the devil thinks he is going to keep hidden from God forever. I remember my friend Lynn say to me, "I am at peace with Jesus now." As a spiritual counselor, there are gentle scriptures, eye contacts, and the overwhelming peace of God in Christ Jesus. I have enjoyed this with patients and their family members.

I want to share these two scriptures with you as I close. I cannot read them without some deep, emotional peace coming over me.

And oh how I pray that for you too. The power of God to change our lives in the difficult moments is not magic. It is majestic and holy and a witness of the interaction between heaven and earth. Maybe I can introduce you interested folks to a relationship with Gabriel.

> For I am convinced that neither death nor life, neither angels nor demons, neither the present nor the future, nor any powers, neither height nor depth, nor anything else in all creation, will be able to separate us from the love of God that is in Christ Jesus our Lord. (Romans 8:38–39 NIV)

> Come to me, all you who are weary and burdened, and I will give you rest. Take my yoke upon you and learn from me, for I am gentle and humble in heart, and you will find rest for your souls. For my yoke is easy and my burden is light. (Matthew 11:28–30 NIV)

To my audience I say, God bless you and amen for now.

Closing prayer: May God be ever so close to you all in your times of need. May the pain of the world yield to the love of God. And may the majesty I know so well sprinkle your soul with the peace of heaven. In the name of the Father, the Son, and the Holy Spirit. Amen.

BIBLIOGRAPHY

The Oxford Theological Dictionary. Philadelphia: Westminster Press, 1983.
Wikipedia.com
The New International Version. Michigan: Zondervan, 2020.
The New King James Version. Nashville: Thomas Nelson Publishers, 1997.
The New Living Translation. Illinois: Tyndale House Publishing, 2007.
The Good News Bible. New York: American Bible Society, 1976.
Swindoll, Charles. *Swindoll's Ultimate Book of Illustrations & Quotes*. Nashville: Thomas Nelson Publishers, 1998.

ABOUT THE AUTHOR

Rev. Richard Stackhouse has served as a pastor and chaplain for over twenty years. He graduated from a bible college in Binghamton, New York, and attended seminary for a year at Drew University in Madison, New Jersey, and three years at Wesley Theological Seminary in Washington, DC. He is an ordained pastor in the Evangelical Methodist Church. He has served in New York, Pennsylvania, Virginia, and Florida as pastor and chaplain.

He is married and has two sons, a stepson, and three grandchildren. They enjoy camping, Bible studies, community worship, and serving God and his people in various ways.